I SEE LIFE THROUGH
ROSÉ-COLORED GLASSES

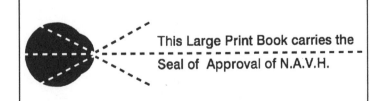

This Large Print Book carries the
Seal of Approval of N.A.V.H.

I SEE LIFE THROUGH ROSÉ-COLORED GLASSES

LISA SCOTTOLINE
&
FRANCESCA SERRITELLA

THORNDIKE PRESS
A part of Gale, a Cengage Company

Farmington Hills, Mich • San Francisco • New York • Waterville, Maine
Meriden, Conn • Mason, Ohio • Chicago

Copyright © 2018 by Smart Blonde, LLC, and Francesca Scottoline Serritella.
All photographs courtesy of the authors.
Thorndike Press, a part of Gale, a Cengage Company.

ALL RIGHTS RESERVED
Thorndike Press® Large Print Core.
The text of this Large Print edition is unabridged.
Other aspects of the book may vary from the original edition.
Set in 16 pt. Plantin.

LIBRARY OF CONGRESS CIP DATA ON FILE.
CATALOGUING IN PUBLICATION FOR THIS BOOK
IS AVAILABLE FROM THE LIBRARY OF CONGRESS.

ISBN-13: 978-1-4328-5249-8 (hardcover)

Published in 2018 by arrangement with Macmillan Publishing Group, LLC/St. Martin's Press

Printed in Mexico
1 2 3 4 5 6 7 22 21 20 19 18

To our beloved Ruby, and to pets
everywhere, because
animals make us human

CONTENTS

I See Life Through Rosé-Colored Glasses

LISA

Welcome to our fun and fizzy collection of stories, taken from our actual lives as a mother and a daughter.

Sometimes we fight.

Sometimes we make up.

And sometimes, yes, we drink.

One of the pleasures of having an adult daughter is that you can share a glass of rosé with her, and by the second one, you forget what you were fighting about.

But that's not the point of this book or its title.

We're not *that* literal.

This is the eighth book in a bestselling series, chronicling our lives, which I bet happens to look like your lives.

If less well behaved.

Like you, we've had our ups and downs, but in this book, we look at the upside of ups and downs.

And that's the meaning of the title.

13

You know how you feel after a few sips of rosé?

That life is good?

That none of your troubles are really that troubling?

That you're lucky just to be alive, to taste something sweet on your tongue, to feel the sun on your face and shoulders, and to share the company of your family, friends, or even your dog or cat?

By the way, animals are family to Francesca and me.

We're both dog- and cat-crazy, and you'd know that as soon as you met us, because lint rollers can only do so much.

Anyway, that rosé feeling is one you can capture even if there's no alcohol in sight.

Anytime you get a moment, or take one, just to pause and savor the simple pleasures.

Of course the best time to do that is in summer, when you're officially allowed to slack for vacation, which turns out to be just more work for Mom, by the seaside.

Still, even a change of scenery can help you exhale, set aside your stress, and take a hiatus from tasks and things-to-do lists.

This book is like that too, and I guarantee that if you take it on vacation, you'll LOL.

For example, I write about what it's like to get older, namely that your eyebrows will vanish and your eyelids acquire hoods. You may look permanently sleepy, but on the plus side, nobody can see the crappy job you did on your eyeliner.

I also write about not being able to zip up my dresses anymore, so now I routinely beg baristas in Starbucks to dress me. And I can't work my jewelry fasteners either, so I only buy necklaces like nooses.

Fun facts about aging!

And Daughter Francesca writes about life as a single thirty-something in New York City. And she has an active dating life, unlike me, who's dead below the waist.

Like I care.

Francesca writes about the light side of dating, and since she's getting older and wiser herself, she's learning to spot the red flags that separate the men from the boys. She's dodged her share of man-bullets, and she's not shy about telling you about them. She even writes about how to break up with a guy, with lots of laughs and better advice than "slip out the back, Jack."

Of course, mothers and daughters may be different, but the similarities are undeniable. Like I write about cleaning out my refrigerator and finding aspirational condiments, and she writes about cleaning out her purse and finding past lives, in her

Handbag Time Machine.

You get the idea.

We take real life and make it funny.

And summer vacation is all about fun. And even if you don't get any vacation, you should read this book, because it'll make you feel like you're on one.

And isn't that the purpose of a book?

To help you escape the everyday.

To make you laugh out loud.

And to make you feel centered and relaxed.

It's like a glass of rosé, between two covers.

Read between the wines.

Pull up a beach chair.

Sit back.

Turn the page.

And take a sip.

Can You Hear Me Now?

FRANCESCA

"Can you hear me now?" is the question my mom and I ask each other most often over the phone, even beating, "What did you have for dinner?"

Do other people talk about food like we do?

I like to know what I'm missing, and my mom needs to know I'm not starving.

For two women who talk *a lot,* we suffer from bad cell-phone reception — and only for our calls to one another. It's like the universe is playing a cruel trick on us, or maybe saying "enough already," but whenever we call each other, the sound cuts in and out.

And every time, we take it personally.

We know the problem is external, and yet we inevitably start blaming each other. It shows the limits of human nature, or at least mother-daughter nature.

I'll be telling my mom a story, and all of a

17

sudden she'll go, "You just cut out, I'm not hearing you."

"Oh no, let me move. Can you hear me now?"

"I hear nothing. Are you there?"

"Can you hear me now? Can you hear me now?" I repeat while running around my apartment, none of which she hears.

"Do you know that I can't hear you? You. Cut. Out," she'll say louder, although I hear her perfectly.

Meanwhile, I'm getting more and more aggravated changing locations and repeating, "can you hear me now?" so that by the time the reception finally returns, I sound like, "ARGH, CAN YOU HEAR ME *NOW*?"

"Hey, don't yell at *me*, I didn't do anything!"

"Ugh, Mom, I *know*, I wasn't yelling at you —"

"Well, that's not a very nice tone! It's not my fault the service is bad, don't get mad at me, be mad at the phone."

"I *AM* MAD AT THE PHONE!"

"BUT YOU'RE YELLING AT ME!"

And we're off to the races. We take turns switching roles, but the script is roughly the same.

Trust me, we've looked into fixing this — changing phones, changing providers, getting a brain-cancer-inducing signal-booster installed in my apartment — but we haven't found an effective and appealing solution.

We're so good at fighting as it is.

I've narrowed down where the service is the worst in my apartment: my kitchen, bathroom, bedroom, and entryway, which leaves me about a hundred square feet, so I call her most often during my dog walks; then our call is interrupted only by people admiring Pip. Attempts to learn where the service is worst at my mom's house have been unsuccessful, because my mom doesn't understand how to check the cell strength.

"Mom, how many bars do you have where you are?"

"What bars?"

"The bars at the top left."

"The Wi-Fi is good, I'm right next to the thingy."

"Not the Wi-Fi, that's the Internet, next to that, the bars beside AT&T."

"Oh, I don't know, it's too small to see."

But our misunderstanding gave me a different idea: FaceTime.

Our cell signal may suck, but the Wi-Fi thingy is strong, and that's all you need for video chatting. Plus, my mom has a theory that our fights over the phone and in the car start because we can't see each other's facial expressions (which are surely beatific and empathy-inducing, definitely not attitudinal or eye-rolling), so FaceTiming should solve that.

She's half-right — because she's usually only half in the frame.

A booming voice cuts through a choir of angels: "And what did you have for dinner?"

FaceTime is supposed to be easy. People do it with babies. But have you ever tried it with an adult mother? I can't seem to teach my mom how to center herself in the camera when we video chat.

For my generation, FaceTime is intuitive. Like all millennials, I went through a secret selfie-certification course where I learned how to find good light, extend my arm, tilt my head at a flattering angle, and keep my fingertips out of the frame.

I have not blinked in a photo since 2007.

If anything, my problem is breaking the habit of looking at myself in the corner window.

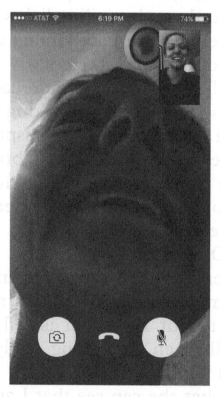

My mom insisted we use this picture in the book.
I tried to dissuade her. But we keep it real!

21

My mother, on the other hand, holds the phone under her chin and talks directly into the microphone, so I'm looking up her nose. Or she holds the phone upright but too high, so I am looking at her forehead.

"Are you looking at my roots?" she'll ask.

"Your roots are all I can see."

In either case, she holds it one inch from her face, so I can check out her pores while we're talking. She could up her moisturizer.

Sometimes she sets the phone down so it points directly at the ceiling lights, and then I get to feel like I'm FaceTiming with God.

Not far off, if you ask Her.

But I will say, we've had more laughs than fights. It's fun; we pull the dogs into the frame and occasionally an unsuspecting cat, I show her new shoes that I bought, she shows me the latest blooms in the garden, and of course, we each show each other what we're cooking.

Call it DinnerTime.

Whatever the technology, communication between mothers and daughters may never be perfect. But my mom is still my first phone call when something really good or really bad happens.

And so that she can see that I ate.

Please Put the Lid Down

LISA

Lately everyone is hating on fake news.

I'm hating on news I wish were fake.

Of course I'm talking about the snake in the toilet.

I read the story on Facebook, source of all reliable news.

I believe everything I read on Facebook, and so should you.

According to Facebook, everyone's marriage is perfect, everyone's children are brilliant, and everyone's vacation is better than yours.

Facebook people live a different life from the rest of us. Their cats are affectionate, their dogs don't poop on the floor, and their meals are photogenic.

They don't eat anything that comes out of a can.

Me, I'm the opposite.

If it doesn't come out of a can, I'm not having it for lunch.

Namely, Amy's soups. Try the Southwestern Chipotle and the Mixed Vegetable.

I change it up for dinner by eating things that come out of jars.

If it doesn't come out of the jar, I cannot be bothered. Rao's spaghetti sauce comes out of a jar, and I can't be the only Italian-American who uses tomato sauce out of a jar.

It's not my secret shame, it's my secret sauce, and who has time to stand in front of a pot all day?

Anyway, to stay on point, it was on Facebook that I read the story of a boy from Texas who woke up in the morning, went to the bathroom, and found a rattlesnake inside his toilet.

I didn't believe it, but there was a picture of a snake coming out of a toilet.

I'm not going to show you because you will never be able to unsee it.

I still think of pictures as proof-positive that something happened, even though nowadays people Photoshop their pictures to look thinner and/or to add or subtract a person.

Like an ex-husband.

I would never Photoshop Thing One or Thing Two out of a picture. Instead I would rip the picture in half, tear the half into pieces, burn the pieces to ashes, jump up and down on the ashes, then sweep the ashes off a cliff.

Which would be so much more satisfying.

But still, the Facebook photo did not look doctored to me at all. On the contrary, it looked exactly like what it purported to be, which was a snake coming out of a toilet.

The story was especially horrifying to me because I'm easy to horrify. I estimate I spend half of my time walking around in horror. I'm horrified by politics, world events, and people who are mean to animals.

Animals never horrify me, except when they come out of toilets.

The other reason this is especially horrifying to me is because I have a garden populated with snakes. I didn't know this until I found a giant ball of snakes rolling around my front yard, which I later found out was a snake mating ball. And the only thing more horrifying than snakes coming out of your toilet is snakes having sex in your front yard.

To return to my point, I went online to verify the snake-in-a-toilet story, and you know what?

The reports agreed that it was possible for a snake to get inside your toilet, but it was unlikely.

Unlikely is not good enough for me.

I need to hear zero possibility.

But nobody is saying that.

On the contrary, *National Geographic* on Twitter stated, "The chances of finding a snake in your toilet are extremely low, but unfortunately not zero."

Now, this is where I reveal that I go to the bathroom to pee approximately thirty-five times a day.

Seventeen of those are at night.

Women pee constantly, and we all know it. That's why the line to the ladies' room is always disproportionately long at any public event, and why some completely frustrated women will get sick of waiting and use the men's room.

(That's me. I'm that woman. No man is ever in there. It's just me, needing to pee. And until the bathroom police come after me, I'm not stopping.)

Anyway, for the past two weeks when I go to the bathroom at night, I cannot bring myself to sit down without checking to see if there is a snake in my toilet. I have to turn on the light, but this wakes me up, so when I go back to bed, I'm nervous and ultimately sleepless.

With no one to blame it on.

Surely not myself.

Maybe Facebook.

Or snakes.

They've been our frenemy ever since they offered Eve the apple.

TRICK QUESTION
LISA

There's something special about an old dog.

No, I don't mean me.

How dare you.

I'm talking about Ruby The Crazy Corgi, who is now thirteen and using her little wheelie cart, since her back legs are paralyzed. This unfortunately means that she's incontinent, so she wears a doggy diaper, but apart from that, she's only gotten better as she's gotten older.

For example, corgis are herding dogs and in her younger days she would try to herd anything in sight, including the other dogs, since we didn't have sheep.

I know, believe me I thought about it.

It would be nice to have a few sheep.

They could live out back like little clouds with feet, and I could have real homemade wool sweaters. This was before I wore fleece constantly, so now I would need them to grow polyester.

In any event, Ruby has learned to stop herding things, since with old age comes the wisdom that we need to not live in constant fear.

Of course she doesn't watch the news.

Lately, I don't either.

Anyway, Ruby isn't the only old dog I've had, since I had a toy poodle named Rosie who lived until the age of sixteen, though for the last five years of her life she was completely blind.

You might be saying aww, but you should be saying, that rocks!

Because the blind years of Rosie's life were her best.

Like Ruby, Rosie had less and less to be worried about, since she couldn't see any of the bad things that she used to see earlier. She settled into a nice comfy contentment, and at the same time, was able to navigate the house with ease, knowing where everything was. The only problem was when I had to take her outside and even that she turned to an advantage. Those were the days when I didn't have a fence in the backyard, so if I put the dogs out, I had to walk them around on a leash.

I did that for fifteen years.

Tell me who the blind one is, am I right?

In any event, I never had to walk Rosie

because as soon as she went blind, when she got out in the backyard, she would walk only in a small circle. This turned out to be the best thing in the world for me, because I never had to walk her, and for her, because she got a ton of exercise. She would just make circles all around the lawn, whatever the weather, and you haven't lived until you've seen yellow circles in your snow.

It was artistic.

And precise.

You would've thought this dog had a protractor.

Some days it looked like the Olympic rings, only one color.

The thing about Rosie in her dotage was that if I left a room, she wouldn't know it, so she had to be picked up and carried from room to room. This isn't as much of a pain as it sounds. First off she only weighed six pounds.

Extremely portable.

I got completely used to picking up something before I left the room, which was excellent practice for the cell phones that would come much later. I swear, part of the reason I never leave my phone anywhere is because Rosie trained me.

We both know that our dogs train us and not vice versa, don't we?

Ruby and her new wheels!

We do all sorts of tricks for our dogs.

Tricks that we never thought we could do, or would ever want to. Like diapering a dog.

Believe me, if you asked me if I would ever put a diaper on a dog, I would've laughed. But now, quite seriously, I'm noticing that more and more she's having a hard time getting around with her front legs in her wheelchair, and I'm facing the notion that Ruby's front legs might become paralyzed too.

Which would leave her with no mobility.

The vet warned me about this a year ago, and I said to myself, if that happens, I might have to make a tough decision.

But that was then, and this is now.

Because now, I don't see any problem at all.

She's otherwise happy and healthy and smarter than ever.

And I'm starting to Google carts for quadriplegic dogs.

Or I can just push her in her cart.

Or carry her from room to room.

Because the thing about a dog is, they never give up on you.

If I had to be carried from room to room, Ruby would carry me.

Rosie would have too.

If you have a dog, you know that is exactly true.

And so Ruby has taught me one final trick.

What are the limits on love?

There aren't any.

It's a trick question.

Do Me a Favor

FRANCESCA

I was leaving a friend's birthday party when I realized I'd left my scarf at the bar. I was going to ask the cabbie to turn around, but we were almost at the Brooklyn Bridge, it would cost time and money to circle back, and I was tired and eager to get home. I don't normally ask for favors, but I thought this one would be easy enough, so I called the birthday boy and asked him to look out for it.

The next morning, he texted me, Hello, hello, I have your scarf.

I was relieved. But it was December 20, and I was about to head out of town for the holiday, so we agreed I would pick it up after Christmas.

January 2, I emailed him with the subject line: "Are you and my scarf free to hang?" It read:

Since you gallantly rescued my scarf, I'll

come to your neighb in Brooklyn so you can just roll outta bed and not be inconvenienced.

And we made plans. But when our Sunday brunch date rolled around, a massive snowstorm had delayed the trains, and what should've been a forty-minute subway ride took an hour and a half with two transfers. I didn't want to be late and make my friend wait, after all, he was doing me a favor, so I got my cardio workout trudge-jogging through the snowy streets.

I finally landed at the restaurant, simultaneously sweaty and cold, with foggy glasses and bleeding heel blisters from my rubber boots — and somehow I still beat him there. But it was fine, I needed the time to defrost. When my friend arrived, we chatted pleasantly over the menus. He didn't mention the scarf.

I didn't want to seem overeager, but when there was a brief lull in the conversation after ordering, I lifted my eyebrows and smiled:

"Do you have my scarf?"

"Oh, yeah, thanks for reminding me," he said, tapping his forehead. I eased back into the booth before he added, "I totally couldn't find it."

"You mean at the bar?"

"No, in my apartment. I know I took it from the bar, but I looked all over this morning, and it's nowhere to be found. I think my cleaning lady must have moved it, I'll have to ask her next time she comes."

"Oh. Okay, thanks, yeah, let me know."

Two weeks later, I hadn't heard from him, so I emailed him again:

Don't mean to be a pest, I just find the longer something is lost, the more likely it is to stay lost.

He said he still hadn't found it, the cleaning lady knew nothing, and offered to buy me a new one. Which was so nice, too nice. I insisted he not do that — I didn't elaborate that it was a lovely tissue cashmere scarf my mother gave me, of greater sentimental and retail value than I could expect him to replace — so I asked only that he keep an eye out for it.

I cursed myself for not simply turning that cab around.

A week later, he texted me a picture of himself holding the scarf! It was hidden in a tote bag, he said.

YAY!!! Thank you, I never doubted you!
We'll coordinate a drop-off next week.

I didn't hear from him again for a month. But again, I couldn't complain, he was doing me a favor! Anyway, a month later, he texted me that he'd be in my area and would drop off my scarf. I wasn't home at the time, but I thanked him and said he could leave it with the front desk.

When I got back to my apartment building, I asked my doorman if a guy had dropped anything off for me. He said yes and retrieved something from the lobby closet and handed me a balled-up piece of fabric.

I shook it out to reveal a wrinkled, leopard-print negligee.

"This isn't mine." I blushed so hard I practically broke into hives. I don't even like when my doormen see me bring a boyfriend home. I'm not in the habit of having them hold my worn lingerie. "This must be for someone else. My friend dropped off a navy blue *scarf*."

My doorman shrugged. "This was what the gentleman left for you."

"Okay, this is a mistake, I'm gonna clear this up. Thanks." I wadded it up into a tight ball. "And he really is just a friend."

My doorman smirked.

I hurried into my apartment, bewildered. Then I texted him.

Bro. This is not my scarf. This is a Victoria's Secret robe, I know you had it, it's in the pic you sent me before!

I added a screenshot of his earlier text with the proof-of-scarf-life photo.

Hahaha omg oops!

He said he grabbed the wrong thing, then added:

Feel free to hang on to the robe — it's an ex's.

Men, amirite?

What woman doesn't want the dirty lingerie of an old girlfriend?

I told him if he didn't want it back, I was going to throw it out.

He didn't like that idea.

Ehh, ok I'll take it back when I swing by later.

And so another round of complex schedule negotiations ensued. I was beginning to worry my scarf had been given to the robeless temptress, when one day I came home, and my doorman again said something had been left for me. I felt residual trepidation, but what could be more embarrassing than a negligee? A naked man?

I mean, I'd take it.

But at long last, it was my scarf! I clutched it to my face in gratitude. It no longer smelled like my perfume, but at least it didn't smell like anyone else's.

I'll never know the secrets of what my scarf had seen or how it had gotten lost, found, lost again, mistaken, and then *finally* found its way home. I only know one thing for certain:

I should've done myself a favor and turned that cab around.

CHRISTMAS WITH THE FLYING SCOTTOLINES

LISA

It's time you knew the truth.

My childhood Christmases were not the norm.

I'm reluctant to tell you because it makes the family look bad.

But I'm a fan of the truth, especially if it's funny.

Here's what happened.

When I was little, The Flying Scottolines were a family of four, living in a tract house in Delaware County, Pennsylvania. But my mother had a very large family and she was the youngest of nineteen children.

Yes, you read that correctly.

Nineteen.

I had eighteen aunts and uncles. Their age span was so large that some were dying while others were being born.

Okay, maybe that's an exaggeration, but not by much.

What does this tell you about my family?

I don't even want to know.

Let's just say they were good Catholics.

Maybe too good.

What does that tell us about my grandmother?

That she had more estrogen than the Northern Hemisphere?

Can you imagine being pregnant nineteen times?

It's like a puppy mill, only with babies.

By the way, my grandmother was married twice. Her first husband died.

You can guess how.

His heart wore out.

Before anything else, evidently.

I would've said, Dude, before bedtime, maybe read a book instead?

Anyway, when I was growing up, most of the aunts and uncles would come to our house for Sunday dinner and on holidays. The house would burst with colorful Italian relatives, like in an Olive Garden commercial but not as well dressed.

Everybody brought potluck, which meant that we had thirty-seven different kinds of pasta.

I adored all of my aunts and uncles, but my favorite was Uncle Mikey, the Fun Uncle.

He drove a convertible Thunderbird, loved

to sing and dance, and did God-knows-what for a living. He loved to play with me and my brother, tickle us, and tell us dumb jokes. But best of all, he always brought us presents on Christmas Eve, like Santa, only smoking a cigarette.

All the other aunts and uncles would give us a Christmas gift by placing them under the tree for us to open on Christmas morning.

But not Uncle Mikey.

He would bring his gifts unwrapped, so we could play with them right away.

Of course, we loved that, as kids.

Delayed gratification was not in our vocabulary.

I always noticed some tension between my parents and Uncle Mikey on Christmas Eve, and one year, the presents from Uncle Mikey stopped abruptly.

Bummer.

I asked my mother why, and that's when she told me that Uncle Mikey's presents "fell off a truck."

Not that that explained anything.

I remember thinking that Uncle Mikey was the luckiest guy ever, always driving around behind trucks full of toys, just when things started falling off the back.

What a guy!

And he must've been the greatest catch, too, because when the toys fell off the truck, he caught them.

Merry Christmas!

Some kids believed in Santa, but I believed in Uncle Mikey.

I didn't care where the presents came from, only that I got them.

Evidently, Uncle Mikey felt the same way.

Then one day, after I had become an adult, I heard the term "fell off a truck" used in a movie. And I learned that it meant the goods were stolen.

Which is when I realized that Uncle Mikey wasn't such a good catch, after all.

No wonder Mother Mary made him stop.

And no wonder the presents were never wrapped.

And no wonder they were always the best.

Because they didn't cost him anything.

The Flying Scottolines were receiving stolen goods.

Luckily we didn't end up behind bars.

And so you get the idea.

That's who we were.

Are you impressed yet?

The truth is never impressive.

It's just real.

And sometimes funny.

THE AD THAT
STOLE CHRISTMAS

FRANCESCA

I was excited for Christmas until Match .com told me I shouldn't be.

The dating website has been running a new TV advertisement entitled, "I Met Someone." The phrase is repeated by different people in different scenarios, but the camera lingers on a final scene at a holiday dinner, where a young woman leans in to an elderly relative and says, "I met someone," to much rejoicing.

Don't do this, Match.com.

Don't turn Christmas into a day to make single people feel bad about being single. Save that for Valentine's Day, New Year's Eve, Fridays and Saturdays.

Let us just have this!

Christmas is pure. It's a holiday for celebration of faith, family, and childlike wonder.

We're celebrating the birth of Christ, a holy infant, an immaculate conception.

And you choose *now* to ask Santa for an online hookup?

Christmas is a perfect time to be single. You go home to your family, binge on all your favorite foods, watch great, old movies, and spend the whole day in pajamas.

Come to think of it, I should try to plan my next breakup for December.

I've been in a relationship over the holidays and I've been single, and honestly, I prefer it this way.

Maybe as a child of divorced parents, I'm already exhausted with splitting the holiday. If you want me to cut the day into thirds, I'm gonna need a ring on my finger.

And a new relationship at Christmas is the worst. The game theory that goes into choosing the perfect gift for a brand-new boyfriend — one that isn't too serious or too jokey, one that neither disappoints nor upstages his gift for you.

I need more liquor in this eggnog just thinking about it.

Single people don't need a TV ad to be reminded we're single at Christmas. 'Tis the season for engagement announcements on social media.

Facebook looks like an emoji-diamond mine right now.

I don't begrudge the happy couples on

my social media feeds. I give my likes, hearts, and double-taps freely.

But I resent that television ad for trying to make us feel like not only are we alone, we're letting our family down.

You're a mean one, Mr. Match.

Also, it's not true. Our older relatives might ask about our dating status, but they're just trying to find something to talk to us about.

Not everyone is caught up on *Game of Thrones.*

If you don't like the line of conversation Great Aunt Bertie is pursuing, look up from your phone and ask her something. Better yet, ask her about her dating life back in the day.

Old ladies have stories.

Maybe that was just my grandmother, Mother Mary. She was very chill about my love life.

One time, I told her I had a boyfriend, and she said, "Why?"

Her sage advice was generally to date around, not get tied down too soon, and not to settle.

She was divorced twice, so she knew a thing or two.

At least two.

I thought of her watching this ad, because

the only scene more manipulative than the holiday dinner was the one where a man is sitting at his grandmother's hospital bedside to tell her, "I met someone," and she's filled with joy and presumably the will to live.

So, not only are single people guilty of ruining Christmas, we're also denying Grandma's final wishes.

Somewhere Mother Mary is laughing.

Because when she fell gravely ill two years ago, I had just ended a long-term relationship, but my uncle advised I not say anything to avoid upsetting her. But later, as I was caring for her in hospice, she asked me about my ex, and I had to tell her the truth.

I told her the whole story, so she'd know that I had tried my very best to make the relationship work. When I was finished, she held up a finger. Speech was difficult for her by then, and when she wanted to make something very clear, she wrote it out on her whiteboard and showed it to me:

"MOTTO — WHO NEEDS IT???"

Then she burst out laughing. We both did.

Mother Mary isn't with us any longer, but I always feel close to her around the holidays. And in my book, she'll always get the final word.

So, sorry, Match.com, you've been overruled. Christmas remains a no-date-needed holiday.

And single or not, if you're lucky enough to spend the day with your family, make sure they feel your love. There's plenty to go around.

A Very Happy New Year

LISA

The holidays are almost over, and you're probably exhausted from cooking, visiting, and pulling pine needles from your toes.

I did all that, but I'm not tired.

You know why?

Drugs.

Not even kidding.

And it's all legal.

Let me explain.

We begin three weeks before Christmas, when I start to get a sore throat. Like every woman during the holidays, I ignore it and soldier on, but my throat gets worse and worse. Every day I think I should call the doctor but I tough it out like a Mommy Martyr.

Yes, mothers make the best martyrs.

It's starts with labor.

Actually, men thought up the name labor, because Torture & Genital Mutilation doesn't look as good on a hospital door.

48

Anyway, I got sick before Christmas, my throat on fire, my head in the proverbial vise, and I felt horrible, head to toe. But of course I waited too long to call the doctor and their offices were closed for the weekend, so I went to Patient First.

A doctor you can see on the spot? Incredible. I have to wait two weeks to get my hair highlighted.

Scottoline First!

Anyway at Patient First, I'm diagnosed with strep throat. They give me antibiotics to go home with, and long story short, I checked in at my regular doctor later, and he prescribed something magical:

Steroids.

As in methylprednisone.

Which cured me instantly.

Or more accurately, made my sickness beside the point. I felt no symptoms at all. My throat felt great, my head cleared, and I went from being sick to well, in a blink.

Holidays, here I come!

Of course, I'm not really advocating drug use, and you're smart enough to know that.

Just say no.

But I didn't, and was highly productive.

I was supposed to take six pills the first day, and by pill two, I had the energy of ten lords a-leaping and nine ladies dancing.

It was like the twelve days of Christmas, chemically enhanced.

I was ready to plant a Christmas tree, grow it, saw it myself, decorate it, and take it down.

I started and finished all my shopping. I signed and sealed all my holiday cards. I wrapped all my gifts. I cleaned the house. I did the laundry. I reorganized my office.

My garden room wasn't completely finished being constructed, but I moved furniture into it anyway. I stopped when I realized that four windows were missing.

I noticed only because the cold blew through my Superwoman cape.

Turns out that steroids are just what I need during the holidays.

It was like the magic pill in *Limitless.*

It's all about Bradley Cooper, isn't it?

I had no idea if my throat hurt because I've never felt so good in my life. It was like a combination of Advil, Robitussin, and crack cocaine.

Per the instructions, I took two of the pills before bedtime, obviously the prescription of Dr. Satan. You can't take two steroids before bed and sleep anytime this century.

I lay wide-awake, but it didn't matter.

I outlined the plots of three novels.

In my head.

Now all I have to do is fill in the blanks.

It's like Mad Libs for the addicted authors.

I admit, I may have been a little edgy, but even that worked for me, like when I lined up the dogs for a Christmas photo and they sat on cue, obeying me for the first time ever.

Nobody wanted to make Holiday Hulk angry.

So bottom line, here we are at the new year, and as you may remember, I don't make resolutions because they're always so negative, as in here's something I hate about myself that I need to change.

I prefer to keep it positive, so I invented unResolutions, in that here's something I like about myself and I resolve to keep doing.

And you know what that is?

Steroids, every December from now on.

Happy New Year!

LOST AND FOUND
LISA

Did you hear the news?

They discovered a new organ.

All this time, it was in your body.

Not even kidding.

Maybe they were looking outside?

Anyway, an Irish surgeon, Dr. J. Calvin Coffey, discovered that we have something in our stomach called a mesentery.

Before now, the mesentery was a mystery.

Dr. Coffey teaches at the University of Limerick, otherwise well known for its limericks.

Like, "There once was a mesentery from Nantucket . . ."

Evidently, the mesentery connects the intestine to the abdomen, and as Dr. Coffey explained, "It keeps the intestine in a particular shape, so when you stand up, your intestine doesn't fall into your pelvis."

Well, hell. That's a good thing.

It's like Spanks for your colorectal system.

Thanks, mesentery!

Meanwhile, I might be in love with Dr. Coffey. He has a way with words. And also if he could find a mesentery, he could find my car keys.

But to stay on point, it turns out that for the past century, medical science had thought the mesentery was a group of disjointed parts, but he figured out it's a connected organ.

Hello!

So now you have an organ you didn't know about.

Like a present you got for the holidays.

And it's just your size!

People don't understand why medical science didn't know about the mesentery before.

Not me. I get it. If I were going to lose something in my body, the most likely place to lose it would be in my stomach.

In the folds.

Above the Bermuda Triangle.

You know what I mean.

All ladies have one, and that's what I call mine. Because any man who goes there is lost forever.

Anyway, if you have stomach folds, you know that they're the reason God made loose sweaters.

That's what I wear to hide my folds, or I avoid sitting altogether.

This is my new thing since my last speaking event, when I sat down and my waistband button popped off, then the zipper went down. I couldn't keep it up. It looked good at the lectern, if you like asymmetrical pants.

Luckily I had on a jacket, which is a folds-hider for special occasions.

And I have other tips for hiding folds.

For example, if you ever see me on the beach, I am lying down. That's the only way my stomach looks flat. Unfortunately, that's when my breasts also look flat, but at least it's a matching set.

Anyway, the thing about folds is that they hide things in addition to mesenteries.

Okay, let's get real.

I happened to look down after a shower the other day, in a rare moment.

It's winter, so the shower is rare.

Also the looking down.

I mean, why? I usually can't see anything over my belly anyway, so who needs that reminder?

Not me.

So when I looked down, my folds smoothed out, and you know what I saw sticking out of my belly button?

Dog hair.

I recognized it because there's dog hair all over my house, and since I have dogs that have yellow, brown, black, and white hair, in every corner is a multicolored canine tumbleweed.

But in my belly button?

Who knew?

Yet, there was, sprouting like a little furry fountain.

I started pulling it out, and the more stuff I pulled out, the more stuff there was, like a magician starts pulling scarves out of a hat.

Not only dog hair, but lint and little shreds of tissue paper.

Who knew what was in there?

Could the Bermuda Triangle be spreading?

Are you horrified yet?

I was. I even got out a tweezers to do the job right, extracting every last foreign object like a surgeon.

In fact, like a surgeon finding a mesentery.

Dr. Coffey, call me.

We have so much in common.

Happy Birthday to Me?

FRANCESCA

Planning your own birthday is a fact of adult life.

Sure, there are years where a best friend or significant other steps up, but in my history, some years I planned it myself.

Okay, every year I've planned it myself.

And every year it makes me completely insane.

I'm well adjusted eleven months out of the year, but when planning my birthday, I become my most neurotic self.

It's agony.

I wish I could be one of those people who is like, "It's mah birthday, bitches!" but I go the opposite direction. I'm filled with anxiety and insecurity over every aspect of it, obsessively concerned that my guests won't have a good time.

It's like I forget they're my friends.

My fantasy is that someone would throw a surprise birthday party for me, but I don't know how anyone would pull it off in real life, because I'm such a nervous planner, I'd beat them to the punch. They'd have to throw it for me two months in advance to save me from the stress spiral that sucks me in each year.

It begins with the venue. I know I should just relax, choose a bar I like, and ask everyone to show up.

But this is a busy city, places get packed, especially on the weekends. I would never want my friends to go out of their way to come to a place of my choosing, only to find there was no room at the bar for them.

So I have to choose a place that will let me reserve space. But what if the space is too large, and I don't have enough friends to fill it? And then the few people who do come will see that I'm actually a loser and rethink our entire relationship.

I evaluate the venue from every angle. Is it cool enough but not trying too hard? Will the menu please everyone from the beer drinker to the cocktail aficionado? Are the drinks overpriced, will it seem too bougie? Is it easy to get to from the subways? If we wanted to go dancing later, are we near a good place for that? Do people other than me even like dancing? Is a second location too much to ask, I mean, how many hours do I expect my friends to devote to celebrating my birth?

Yelp is my spiral-enabler. The Internet provides us too much information for our own good. I lose hours scouring reviews containing the words "birthday party" for every potential bar or lounge, and one bad experience crosses it off the list.

I'm like a codependent Goldilocks. "Is this bed okay for you? Do you have a preferred sleep number? Just let me know, I can change it!"

Inevitably, I take so long finding the place that is just right, when I call it's already booked.

Luckily I have four more on standby.

Then there are the invitations. You would think as a writer, this would be the most comfortable part for me. Think again.

I spend my professional life thinking about my "voice" in writing, and I can't turn that off for crafting the invite. I go through drafts before I send anything out.

I thought Paperless Post was the answer to my prayers, because it gave me less room to write. But there are pages upon pages of options. At first it starts out fun to browse the pretty designs, but soon it devolves into an identity crisis of the Millennial era:

What flavor of hipster whimsy am I?

Am I an ironic rainbows and unicorns person? Vintage wallpaper florals? Childhood photo of myself looking weirdly precocious?

My options for that last one are limited, as my mom used to cut my bangs.

When in doubt, I generally settle for something with booze on the cover.

(See this book jacket.)

I save the hardest part of the birthday planning for last: the cake.

First, a tough question: am I too old to want a *birthday cake*?

I mean, I *do* want cake, pretty much all the time. A birthday is a rare occasion when adults get to eat cake without shame. And that provides me the loophole to ordering one — I tell myself I'm doing it for my guests and not my insatiable appetite for refined sugar.

But something about ordering my own birthday cake feels pathetic, like sending yourself flowers.

Between dignity and cake, I choose cake.

So I call up the fabulous bakery near me to place an order. Early on, it's still plausible that I'm ordering this for someone else's birthday — based on my choices, pink frosting and red writing, perhaps a small child's. The moment of truth comes when they ask me: "What do you want it to say on it?"

Is "I am alone" too dark?

In the past, I've gritted my teeth and asked for *Happy Birthday, Francesca,* hoping they didn't match the name to my credit card.

This year it finally occurred to me that it didn't need to say anything — although I forget that my friends actually like me, I remember they know my name — so I opted for a round cake with icing ripples on top.

"Do you want disco dust on it?" the baker asked.

"Excuse me?"

"It's really fine, edible sparkles on the top."

"This is for my thirty-first birthday," I confess, expecting a gasp of horror on the line, but he says nothing. So I venture, "Does it look good?"

"It looks *awesome.*"

"I'm not too old for it?"

"No, girl! I would get this on my birthday cake, too!"

For the first time in the planning process, I was having fun. "Okay, yes! And while you're at it, make the inside funfetti cake."

"YAS!"

When the planning is done and my party rolls around, I always have a good time.

Each year I'm reminded that my friends are easygoing and wonderful, and I kick myself for fretting so much. I am genuinely lucky to plan any occasion that gets all of these fantastic people in a room together. If that takes some extra stress, it's well worth it.

And when I finally mellow out enough to give my friends a chance to help me, they don't let me down. This year, without my asking, my friend took charge of the candle lighting and got everyone singing. When they brought it over for me to blow the candles out, a huge smile spread across my face.

The disco dust was totally worth it.

To Boldly Go

LISA

You've probably heard that we discovered seven new planets that might have water.

Good, because I'm thirsty.

You probably are, too.

Everybody's thirsty all the time, that's why we're always carrying bottles of water around that we have to throw somewhere.

But no worries.

Soon we'll have new planets to throw our water bottles around on.

This is great because it's getting cluttered down here, with the trash and all. There are landfills of trash, Dumpsters of trash, and lakes of trash. There's even a floating island of trash that's sailing around the ocean, like a cruise with really bad food.

It takes a long time to throw enough crap around to mess up an entire planet, but I think we're finally getting there.

And now that we're just running out of planet to throw things around on, just in time, we discover there are seven new planets to throw things around on.

Some species have all the luck.

The new planets have their own system, called TRAPPIST-1, which sounds like a vanity plate to me. Considering what we're going to do to them, maybe we should change the name to TRASH-IT.

And if you ask me, time's a wastin'.

Those planets aren't going to trash themselves.

They need experts to do it for them, and we're already behind the eight ball.

Luckily, I think we have the learning curve down. I don't expect it will take us as long to trash those planets as it did this one, plus there are more people making more trash every day, so hopefully if we all pitch in, we can get this job done in no time.

We are the world.

And we trash it together.

I have the same exact problem with my kitchen drawers.

They keep getting filled up but it's a pain in the neck to clean them out. I would love it if I had a whole new set of drawers to junk up.

Sometimes you just have to start over.

It's like divorce for your planet.

The way I see it, I have two ex-husbands

but only one ex-planet. So I'm behind the count.

Or ahead?

That goes for digging, too.

We've done a lot of digging and we're running out of places to dig. In fact about five years ago, we dug in the bottom of the ocean and we made a hole in the planet and the stuffing came out.

Oops.

You remember when that happened. We had to plug the hole, but nobody's fingers were big enough, so we were in real trouble.

To me, the solution was simple.

Eat more.

Then your fingers will get chubbier and pretty soon you'll be able to plug any hole you want to.

I figured that out all by myself.

You didn't know I was that smart, did you?

Anyway I'm excited about our new planets, which already have their own website. You can't blame them. If those planets want us to fly up there and start trashing, they have to promote themselves.

The competition will be fierce.

But I think we're up to the challenge.

After all, we put the first man on the moon.

Isn't it about time we put the first Dumpster everywhere else?

Not only that, but I bet there are a lot of cool new animals we've never seen before up there.

We definitely need new animals, since we're almost out of them down here. More and more animals are disappearing every day. All creatures great and small, until they're so small, they're gone.

Well, that's not exactly true. To clarify, we have too many dogs and cats, but we don't have enough giraffes or lions.

This is because their heads keep ending up on people's walls.

If only they could keep their heads, then they would live.

You need a head to live.

Again, I'm a genius.

Ask me anything.

That's why I'm hopeful that if we get to these new planets, those animals will have heads and they'll be around longer.

Also you need a head to breathe.

Oxygen.

There are places that are running out of oxygen on this planet, so we need to go where the oxygen is, on our new planets.

We'll have to fly there.

Unfortunately, it's far away. According to the website, it will take thirty-nine light-years to get there. So we'll need a lot of snacks.

And a lot of gas.

Which might make some smoke.

But the smoke will clear up in time, like maybe 5 million years, and by then we will have discovered another seven new planets.

It will all work out in the end, don't you think?

It always has.

It always will.

In another world.

Oh Captain, My Captain

LISA

I'm back from yet another adventure in flying.

And I'm happy to report that everyone survived, including me.

We begin when I find myself on one of those commuter flights, which I hate because I'm afraid to fly.

And there's nothing like a small plane to remind you of your own mortality.

Because there's nothing underneath the plane except the earth.

At something of a distance.

Usually I confide in the flight attendant that I'm afraid to fly, and they always tell me that air travel is safer than being on a road, that some turbulence is normal, and that the captain has everything under control.

Generally I take comfort in that response, until this particular flight, when the captain seemed less than reliable.

Let me explain.

Because I'm so paranoid about flying, I begin checking everything, even in the jetway. I always make sure that the jetway meets the plane exactly, so that there's no gap. I do this because I read that once there was a gap and somebody fell through it onto the tarmac and died.

So I'm all over the jetway-gap issue.

By the way, I never worry about terrorists. I leave that to government agencies. I can't do everything and I've got my eye on that jetway gap.

Then I go on board the plane and before I sit down, I check the cockpit. I make sure that the pilots don't look too old, too young, or too drunk.

Because I read an article about drunk airline pilots, so I conduct field sobriety tests.

To wit, I always make a point of saying hello to the pilots, so they'll have to say hello back.

I want to smell their breath.

If it smells like onions, terrific.

If it smells like vodka, less so.

And if they don't say hello back, I ask them a question, like:

"How are you?"

"Do you expect any turbulence?"

"Are you single?"

Just kidding.

I never ask that.

I only think it.

Laugh all you want to, but if you're on one of my flights, you have me to thank for getting home safely.

Anyway, on the flight in question, I saw the pilot and asked him, "How are you?"

He answered: "Tired and cranky."

His breath was fine.

His answer wasn't.

I forced a smile, though I was really thinking, How tired?

And how cranky?

And believe it or not, I wasn't the only one thinking these things, because the next thing that happened is that somebody on board had a medical issue, which provoked discussion between the pilots and the flight attendants on how to solve the problem, and all the passengers eavesdropped and heard the tired-and-cranky pilot bossing around the other pilot and the flight attendants.

In a very tired and cranky way.

So while the tired-and-cranky pilot went off to deal with the medical issue, I asked the guy next to me, "Does the pilot seem depressed to you?"

The guy answered, "You mean Mr. Job Satisfaction?"

I laughed. "That's Captain Job Satisfaction to you, sir."

Then he laughed.

But we were both nervous, and all of us passengers started looking at each other wondering. Because we all read the article about that pilot in Switzerland flying people into a mountain, and I prefer to die another way, perhaps at the mall, and not just yet.

So if you know me, you know what happened next.

I called the flight attendant over and asked her if the tired-and-cranky pilot was going to fly us into a mountain.

That's right.

I said it.

I no longer edit myself.

If I'm worried, guaranteed I'm going to worry *you.*

She answered, "No, he'd never hurt anybody."

Great.

I thought about getting off the flight, but I ordered a drink instead.

In the end, we landed safely.

And I was the one with the vodka breath.

THE CAKE HAS SPOKEN

FRANCESCA

Every relationship has that moment when the clouds of self-delusion part to reveal with stark clarity: this relationship is over.

For me, it was looking down at my birthday cake.

If that seems to you like a strange time for an epiphany, I agree. But with an emotion as grand and mysterious as love, sometimes it takes a moment of utter banality to snap reality into focus.

They say love is blind, but I think when we want to fall in love, we tie the blindfold ourselves. When you want a relationship to work, you try to explain away potential issues, block out bad arguments, or avoid incompatibilities entirely. In my relationship history, I've skated by red flags like they were obstacles on a ski slalom. And once I'm committed, I've smiled through the embarrassment of a public fight, forgiven cheating, and once even denied to myself

71

that I felt physical fear — not for the long term, but in the moment, I couldn't react the way I needed to. It's hard to process things when emotions are high, and we're not always ready to pull the plug that instant.

But then, in the quiet of everyday life, something small makes it all click.

My mom tells a story about when she knew she had to end an engagement with a man between Thing One and Thing Two. We lived with him when I was three or four, and I liked him, though I was happy when we moved out. From my little-kid perspective, he was nice but very strict. When I was older, my mom explained more to me, and I completely agree she made the right decision for her and us. But she says that the moment it crystallized for her was looking at his shoe trees.

"I was putting clothes away in his closet, and I saw all his shoes with their wooden shoe trees lined up, and I swear, the shoe trees spoke to me, and they said, 'Save your own life.'"

Were the shoe trees a metaphor for his controlling nature? A voice of warning from the other side? A mothball-induced hallucination? She can't say for sure. But all she knows was that those shoe trees spoke to her, and in that moment, she decided to break things off.

Which brings me to my own lightbulb moment occurring over a high-calorie baked good.

Cake really is a girl's best friend.

I had been seeing this guy for several months, and I was on the fence. After an initial period of infatuation, our momentum had slowed. He was good-looking, smart, accomplished, and gentlemanly. He could also be moody, shy, and defensive. I negotiated with myself constantly, stuck in the limbo of a teetering pros-cons list in my mind, fearing deep down that we didn't seem to be falling in love but unable to let go of the exciting potential we showed early in the relationship.

We *should* be a perfect match, I said to myself, and we *were* so great in the beginning, *if we could just get back to that . . .*

(Back to the glorious time of not knowing.)

It's easy to rush into a relationship with the idea of someone. It's a little harder to make it work with an actual human being.

My birthday came faster than I could make up my mind, so I tabled the decision and hoped with age would come wisdom. It did, but not in the way I thought.

The night of my birthday party was his debut to my entire friend group. It went . . . okay. He looked handsome and was attentive, announcing himself as The Boyfriend with plenty of small back touching. But later in the night, he got edgy with a couple girlfriends of mine, wading into political disagreements and generally sticking with arguments past the point of being funny. I came to the rescue before things got really awkward. I was embarrassed, but I didn't want to let it ruin the night.

Apparently it already had.

Mere moments after I waved good-bye to my last birthday guest, I learned that he was furious with me. He said I didn't have his back and accused me of making him look bad in front of my friends.

It took me completely by surprise. I'd honestly thought I'd defused the situation with a joke after he'd behaved boorishly; in my mind, I had covered for him. From his perspective, he was the victim and I had piled on. I was genuinely sorry his feelings were hurt and I didn't want to fight, so I apologized and reassured him that none of my friends thought he was a bad guy.

Jury was out on what I thought.

So we made up, went home, and put the *agida* behind us.

We were cuddling in my bed, when he asked me if I had any cake left. I told him it was in the kitchen, and he scampered off for a midnight snack. I rolled over and went to sleep.

The next morning, like always, things looked brighter. I entered the kitchen, put on a pot of coffee, and thought I deserved a little sugar. I got a small plate for a piece of cake.

I opened the cake box, and it was like a slap in the face.

Inside, what had once been a neat third of a beautiful cake now looked like a bear had clawed out the center of it. Only a raggedy husk remained, an icing-crusted fork sticking out of its heart like a stake.

My boyfriend padded in sleepily.

"Did you . . . do this?" I asked.

"I had some last night, remember?"

"Right, but, why didn't you cut yourself a slice?"

He shrugged and smiled impishly.

"And you ate all these chocolates, too?" Beside the cake was a similarly ravaged box of caramels my best friend in London had sent me. I hadn't even opened it before he got to it; he'd literally had to remove the ribbon and plastic.

"Now you're making me feel bad."

"I'm not, I'm just . . ."

My gaze fell back down to the cake. And I knew.

I am truly my mother's daughter, because that birthday cake said to me, "This man is angry at you. He's not going to love you, he might not even like you. And be honest, you feel the same way."

He pulled out a chair at my table. "So, what's for breakfast?"

"I'm all out." Of . . . breakfast food? It didn't even make sense. I meant it more metaphorically than I understood at the time. "I have to meet my dad for brunch, so . . ."

"Oh, sure, yeah, I uh, I gotta go anyway."

So he knew, too.

We broke up for good two days later.

To be sure, I sent photos of the cake carcass to my mom and three different girlfriends. The verdict was unanimous; his spite-eating was a message that could not be denied.

The cake had spoken.

Like a good friend, carbs will always tell you the truth.

A Very Special Delivery

LISA

I get lots of junk mail.

But now I'm getting mail about my junk.

No kidding.

Fair warning, this is going to get personal, which you could have guessed.

Unless you're new around here.

That was a trigger warning for middle-aged people.

Because what I got in the mail was a do-it-yourself colonoscopy kit.

I know, right?

So much is wrong with that sentence I don't know where to start.

So let me back up.

Heh heh.

And before I start kidding around, let me say that I understand completely colorectal cancer is a deadly, horrible disease. Everybody should get tested for it, and thank God it can be detected early. That speech should go without saying, and rest assured that I'm just a nice lady who's trying to make you laugh.

So to return to my point, yesterday I went to my mailbox, which was stuffed with catalogs I didn't want, flyers for products I'll never order, and offers for services I don't need. In other words, junk, junk, junk. I toss it directly into the recycling bin. The companies should address the mail to my recycling bin and save us all the time.

The last thing in my mailbox was a thick envelope that I didn't recognize, so I opened it up and inside were several letters and a small plastic vial with a mint-green top. The cover letter was from my health insurance company, and it read:

Dear Valued Member, Enclosed is an at-home fecal immunochemical test (FIT) for colorectal cancer screening.

Wait, what?

My health insurance company values me?

That's a surprise.

They've been giving me the shaft for years.

Anyway, who knew there was such a thing as a do-it-yourself colonoscopy kit?

I love to do things myself, but there are exceptions to every rule.

I know people whose head is up their ass, but I'm not one of them.

And I like to do things myself, but not my

own colonoscopy.

What will they send me next?

A knife for heart surgery?

Duct tape to plug up that leaky valve?

Also, I had no idea why I got mailed a do-it-yourself colonoscopy kit. I hadn't ordered it. I like free things in the mail, but why is it never chocolate cake? Or a credit toward my health insurance bill?

Then I realized that it was probably something they send to people of a certain age. For example, nobody's sending me an at-home pregnancy kit.

Evidently, there's a big difference between the age group for number one and for number two.

If you follow.

I mean, Big Brother really is watching.

With a microscope.

Where the sun don't shine.

It's spooky to think that strangers are keeping track of my colon.

It's not the Deep State. It's the Deep, Deep State.

I wonder if they know that I gained three pounds. Or that I still take a safety pin to the occasional zit.

You read that right.

Dr. Scottoline is in.

And it works.

Meanwhile, if they send you a do-it-yourself colonoscopy kit when you're sixty years old, what do they send you when you're ninety?

A coffin?

Anyway, you get the idea. Evidently, I was supposed to go to the bathroom, read the directions, and give myself a colonoscopy.

How did we get here?

You know it started in grocery stores, after they started making us check ourselves out.

It was a slippery slope, folks.

We should have nipped that in the bud.

Or the butt.

But here it is, biting us in the you-know-what.

Anyway, according to the instructions, I was supposed to "deposit my stool sample" on the "supplied collection paper," which is a euphemism for the high-end toilet paper they sent in the kit.

Meanwhile, are you still with me?

Or did you barf already?

That was how I felt.

I pick up dog poop all day. But my own, I generally like to keep that at arm's length.

Well, evidently after I collect the sample, I have to put it in the vial, which would be a neat trick because the vial is really small.

If you've ever seen the inside of one of my

jelly jars, you can see the problem.

And there's no knife to wipe off on the rim.

And we ain't talking strawberry jam.

Then evidently, I'm supposed to put the vial into a red biohazard bag.

I would've preferred pink, but nobody asked.

Or, more accurately, brown.

We oldsters need all the visual cues we can get.

And then I'm supposed to mail this lovely package back in another envelope they provided.

Which is the good news.

I get to send my health insurance company back what they've been sending me.

You've got mail!

WITH A CHERRY ON TOP

LISA

I just completed an emotional journey.

I cleaned out my refrigerator.

Let me explain.

I finished a draft of my next book, which means that writer hell is behind me, until I get the letter from my editor suggesting changes to the manuscript.

I'm not complaining.

I love my editor. Her edits improve my books, and she's the only person in the world I take orders from.

So every time I finish a manuscript, I feel like the decks have been cleared, and for a day or two, I find myself cleaning everything in sight.

I started with the refrigerator.

You can guess why.

It's where I spend most of my time.

Yet I'm capable of ignoring parts of it for long periods, and when I started to clean it out, I realized how long.

You don't want to know.

Or maybe you do, and now you'll find out.

I wiped down the main part of the refrigerator, which was reasonably clean, but then I started to look at the shelves on the door. There are four of them, with bottoms that used to be transparent before they were covered with maple syrup, Worcestershire sauce, and a yellow liquid I can't identify.

No, not that yellow liquid.

Okay, maybe.

Plus they were so full that the upside-down ketchup bottle had to be jammed in.

By the way, I'm a big fan of the upside-down ketchup bottle.

Whoever thought of that was a genius.

I spent an entire childhood smacking the bottom of a glass bottle and hoping for the best.

Every bottle in the world should be made upside down, but I digress.

I started to look at my shelves and I thought, why do I have so much stuff?

There's only one of me, and I'm short.

So I went through the jars and bottles to see what they were and why I was keeping them. They were:

Maraschino cherries, from the time I was going to make Manhattans and never did.

Capers, from the time I was going to make

a fancy salmon dish and never did.

Baby gherkin pickles, from the time I was going to make a special appetizer and never did.

You get the idea.

My condiments are aspirational.

They're for the festive fancy life I want to lead, but don't.

They live in a Williams-Sonoma catalog.

I do not.

They entertain frequently.

I nap frequently.

The question was whether I keep the aspirational condiments or throw them away.

At first I couldn't decide, even though I've never ever used any of them.

The only condiments I ever use are ketchup, mustard, A-1 sauce, and sweet relish, because all of those taste great on top of a veggie burger, which I microwave.

We're talking haute cuisine.

Or haute mess.

It goes without saying that all of the aspirational condiments were past the expiration date.

But that never stops me.

I regard expiration dates as negotiable.

Guidelines, not laws.

So at first, I didn't want to throw them away.

I wanted to keep my hopes and dreams alive.

That lasted a haute minute.

I ditched them.

Sayonara, hopes and dreams.

That's the story of being middle-aged.

Realizing that the maraschino life will never be yours.

Because the one you have is much better.

Who needs capers when you have freedom, fun, and the ability to not try so hard anymore?

I think that's called perspective.

And I learned it from the relish.

Either way, I couldn't be happier.

And then there was another whole category of condiments that are unique to me.

And maybe you.

My neighbor used to make berry preserves and give me one every holiday season. She called it Paradise Jelly, and she gave it to me every year, in an adorable jar with a red ribbon. I have three jars on the refrigerator shelves, and when I wiped them down, I realized that she stopped making Paradise Jelly nine years ago, which was the last time she gave me one.

So there you have it.

Every nine years, I clean out my refrigerator shelves.

Whether they need it or not.

Don't eat at my house — or maybe you should.

If my refrigerator gets you sick, it's growing the penicillin to cure you.

But I wasn't sure what to do with the Paradise Jelly.

Did I keep it or throw it away?

Are you kidding?

Of course, I kept it.

It's a condiment with sentimental value.

Nine years from now, I bet I'll do the same thing.

And this is where I tell you that in the freezer, I have a Tupperware container of meatballs in gravy, from Mother Mary.

I can't bring myself to eat it.

But I'm sure as hell not throwing it away.

NSF NYFW

FRANCESCA

The reality of Manhattan life rarely matches up with the fantasy on TV, which fails to convey the pee smell, but last week I was living the dream when I went to a party at New York Fashion Week.

I was invited by a friend from high school who is now a high-powered PR agent in fashion. She must remember me as cooler than I am.

I felt confident enough to accept because I'd just had my hair cut. As anyone with unruly hair knows, you need to honor the blowout.

I might've felt unworthy, but my hair deserved this.

But what would I wear? I ran my first outfit idea by my friend in a text message. Her reply:

☹

"Dressier?" I asked.

She sent a screenshot of the guest list full

of top models and celebrities, along with the word "peak."

I promised I wouldn't embarrass her, but inwardly, I panicked. What did I have in my closet that was "peak"? Put bluntly, what did I have that was both recently dry-cleaned and still fit?

Questions Anna Wintour never needs to ask.

I worried about finding the party address, but there was an honest-to-goodness red carpet. The photographers lowered their cameras to give me the live version of the blank face emoji.

I didn't take it personally. Instead, I weaved through them, hunched and apologetic, as if I were walking in front of a movie screen. I was so hasty exiting the carpet, I completely missed the coat check and had to carry my bulky puffer jacket.

No one should have to be fashionable in February.

The event was as glamorous as I'd imagined. A handful of select, emerging designers were featured, beautiful clothes and accessories on display — tough leather skirts and architectural jackets, stylish *chapeaux* and vintage watches, glittering heels and embroidered-silk slippers.

If I'd been able to sit down in my dress, I

would've tried the shoes on.

As I'd anticipated, my friend was too busy hosting to hang, but it was fun to see her in professional mode. She looked gorgeous and confident as she worked the room, seamlessly shifting between warm interactions with party guests and deft directions to staff.

The only downside — I was on my own.

I'd been anxious that everyone would have runway bodies and I'd feel like some writer-ogre, but the crowd was beautifully diverse. In some ways, it looked like any other industry party, except there were more women, better, mostly black clothing, and a shared love of a bold lip.

They could maintain carefully lined, burgundy lips because few were eating. Servers circulated with trays of hors d'oeuvres that the attractive guests politely refused.

This was when I leaned in to my writer identity and sampled every treat that came by — for research!

In my industry, a sample size is eight and a half by eleven.

Without shame, I flagged down my favorite server for round two of the mini ice-cream pops. My mouth was full or I would've explained, "I work at home."

Honestly, you couldn't get fat on this food if you tried. The portions were comically small. One appetizer was styled to look like a potted plant, with a tiny heirloom carrot served in a thimble-sized clay pot of hummus.

A baby carrot would be too large a serving. These carrots were prenatal.

Baby carrots and hummus made to look like a tiny potted plant. Fashion industry portion control.

The open bar, however, was serving Big

Gulps. My Pinot Grigio came filled so high, I had to slurp the brim.

Tiny bite, generous pour — fashion's food pyramid.

Maybe it was the booze, but I started to relax and enjoy myself. Networking events can be great when it's not your job field. I got to admire the designers' work and meet people without pressure to "connect." My sole objective was not to spill on the clothes.

In the end, I only spilled some on my own.

As the party wound down, some people I'd met asked me to join them for after-party drinks downtown. I looked for my pal, but she'd been hustling nonstop, so I figured I wouldn't interrupt her flow and gave her a little wave from across the room.

Outside, we were just about to get in a cab when my friend came jogging out. "You're leaving?"

"I wanted to say good-bye, but they said you'd join us later, and —"

She stopped me with a giant hug. "Thank you for coming."

I was touched.

I guess you can still use an old friend, even at the peak.

WOMEN'S HISTORY MONTH
LISA

March is Women's History Month, and we're celebrating women everywhere.

Even on Brawny paper towels.

Yes, the Brawny package used to have a superhot guy standing with his arms folded, but now there's a superhot dark-haired woman with her hands on her hips.

We took his job and his red plaid shirt.

I'm sure this is what you were hoping for, as a woman.

To be a corporate spokesmodel dressed like a couch.

I was so intrigued by this that I went to the company website, where a banner says, "The Brawny Man Is Stepping Aside to Celebrate Women."

What a (Brawny) Man!

This would probably be the fastest way that women advance, taking nonpaying jobs from cartoon characters.

And what woman doesn't want to be

identified as brawny?

I myself lie awake at night, hoping that someday I will find a man to whisper in my ear, "Lisa, you are so . . . brawny."

Actually in honor of Women's History Month, the company should have changed the name of the paper towels to Busty.

I'd rather be Busty than Brawny. You might too. Push-up bras and breast implants sell for a reason.

Pass me those Busty paper towels.

They do double the work.

And they're soft!

On the website, the campaign has a slogan, which is, "The strength to take on tough messes."

The perfect description of my second marriage.

If your messes can be cleaned up with a paper towel, they're not messy enough.

To clean up a truly tough mess, you need a lawyer.

Plus I've never relied on a paper towel to give me strength.

I have chocolate for that.

The campaign even has its own hashtag: #StrengthHasNoGender.

I knew that already. I was raised by #MotherMary, who was definitely full strength.

I bet your #Mom is, too.

And so are you, thank God.

On the Brawny website is a coupon that says, "We're not giving you a discount. You earned it."

Is that butch enough for you?

We women don't need no stinking discounts.

We're discounted enough. Often. Everywhere.

Sorry, I don't think that's what they meant.

Also in honor of Women's History Month, the website says: "Every time a woman shatters expectations and norms, there's another woman ready to break through another barrier."

Look, let's be real. That's like saying: "Women. There's more where that came from."

Or, "Women. They love to break things."

Or finally, "Women. The more things they break, the more messes they make, and the more paper towels you need. So buy Brawny towels for all of your messes-created-by-women needs!"

Plus I wonder what this all means for Mr. Clean.

He might have to step aside for Ms. Clean. Which would be a shame because he just got a new butt.

Yowza.

Have you seen him in the commercials? His paper towels would be called Booty.

Mr. Clean looked damn good sweeping the floor. Or maybe the sight of a man doing housework qualifies as pornography.

I saw that commercial during the Super Bowl and I was so distracted by Mr. Clean in his tight pants that I forgot I was supposed to be watching the football players in their tight pants.

I love sports!

But I don't think Mr. Clean will lose his job to Ms. Clean, not if she has to wear his outfit. No woman thinks she looks good in white. I'd look like The Great White Whale.

Now I'm thinking that Mr. Clean should date the Brawny Lady.

Swipe right, Mr. Clean.

And sweep right, too.

Now bend over.

Sorry, I got distracted.

Mr. Clean and the Brawny Lady would be a match made in corporate heaven. They could get married and produce household products with questionable promotional campaigns.

But Mr. Clean better move fast. The Brawny Lady is going to be gone soon. The company says their girlpower paper towels are only a Limited Edition.

Women's History Month will be history.

But the good news is, we women will go on.

In fairness to Brawny, their website does celebrate heroic women like Harriet Tubman and Amelia Earhart. They were great, but I also celebrate women like us. Who don't fly around the world, but show strength every day, in every way.

Whether you head a family or a company, whether you're single or you're married, you're writing your own life story every day.

Even if you don't make history books, you're making your own history.

You're influencing more people than you know. Everyone who loves you will remember you after you're gone. They will remember things you did and said. The proof is that every one of us can recall some saying of our mothers.

Just like I remember Mother Mary's.

She always said, Be yourself, honey.

And I am.

So be yourself and make your own history.

You're my heroine.

Dr. Lisa, Roving Relationship Expert
LISA

I'm a relationship expert.

Ask me anything.

Just not why I'm divorced twice.

The thing is that when you get to be my age, you start to think that you're an expert in many things, including relationships.

Other people's relationships, of course.

Even when the other people are complete strangers.

In other words, I have you pegged even though I don't know you.

This is called wisdom, perspective, and experience.

Or just being a know-it-all.

That's what Mother Mary used to call me. "Don't be such a know-it-all," she would say.

But I couldn't help it.

Because I. Know. It. All.

All moms do.

Mother Mary was a know-it-all, too.

Mother Mary, the OG Know-It-All!

Take it from me, the only people who call you a know-it-all are other know-it-alls who think they know even more than you, which is impossible since there is no more than *all*.

Anyway nobody uses the term "know-it-all" anymore.

Now we have Google, so everybody knows-it-all.

Or conversely, nobody knows anything and relies on a computer to know-it-all.

Anyway, to come to my story, I was at the movies with my best friend Franca on Saturday night, as is our custom. We usually meet an hour early before the show so we can talk. And of course at that time, no one else is in the theater, as was the case this Saturday night, when we went into the theater, sat down, and talked among ourselves, quite happily.

There was nobody else in the theater for the longest time, until a young couple came in and sat in our row, about six seats away. We had assigned seats, since it was a cushy theater with big seats, which we love.

Correction, which our butts love.

The only thing on the screen was ads for local businesses, since we were so early it wasn't even time for previews. So we ignored the ads, but evidently, we couldn't be ignored.

Because the guy in the couple shouted over to me, "Would you please stop talking?"

I looked over, confused. I'm super-courteous at the movies, never talking or checking my phone. "It's just the ads. We won't talk during the movie or the previews."

"I told you to shut up, so shut up."

DUDE, RESPECT YOUR ELDERS.

No woman in the world likes being told to shut up, especially not one with sixty-one-year-old ovaries.

I said, "We're talking quietly. We're allowed to have a conversation."

"You're ignorant!" he said.

I should have said, *On the contrary, I'm a know-it-all.* But I didn't.

Instead I said, "No, *you're* ignorant," which is an embarrassing comeback for a professional writer, but whatever.

"You *better* stop talking."

"*You* better leave us alone."

Mind you, this was a completely empty movie theater except for Franca, me, this jerk, and the young girl whose life he must make miserable. I would have moved but for the assigned seats. He may have felt the same way. We were prisoners of Fandango.

But he shouted, "I can't believe you're not going to stop talking!"

"I can't believe that you don't believe that! Now leave us alone and we'll agree to disagree!"

I turned to Franca to resume our conversation, but both of us had forgotten what we were talking about, since we're both sixty-one.

Then the previews started, and we had wasted our fun talking time.

Which brings me to the relationship part.

All I could do during the movie was think of that girl in the couple. She went red during the shouting match and at one point, she even covered her face with her hands.

I don't know if she was embarrassed by him or by me, but let's be real.

Who would be embarrassed by me?

I'm adorable.

Anyway I felt terrible for her. She was young and cute, and she could be with a man who wasn't trying to control the entire universe.

Much less me.

Good luck with that, sir.

I will cut you *for sport.*

So at the end of the movie, being a relationship expert, I wanted to warn the girl. I wanted to tell her not to marry that guy, if she hadn't yet. As the credits rolled, I told Franca about my great idea, that I wanted to go offer unsolicited advice to a total stranger. I was on a rescue mission for someone who might not want rescuing.

Franca advised against. "Don't, honey. It will just start a fight."

And I said, "Or it might finish one."

But Franca was right as usual, and I didn't do anything.

To a certain extent, I've been that woman.

The woman cringing instead of getting out.

It took me awhile to get out, but I did and I'm happy every day. I always remember that quote by the late Robin Williams: "I used to think that the worst thing in life was to end up alone. It's not. The worst thing in life is to end up with people who make you feel alone."

And now this is always my relationship advice.

Get out.

It was even the title of the movie that we were seeing that night:

Get Out.

When the universe tells you something, listen.

IF YOU WANT
SOMETHING DONE RIGHT
FRANCESCA

I just lost an hour going down a YouTube rabbit hole, only this time I did it on purpose.

I'm learning how to groom my dog.

Not the average de-matting and nail-clipping. I already brush Pip every night like he's my pretty, pretty princess. I even brush his teeth (sometimes). But now, I'm looking to take my pet care to the next level:

I will attempt to give my dog a full-body clip.

Ideally without making him look like *Dog, Interrupted.*

I've always paid a professional to do Pip's summer cuts. But lately, I've observed how he dreads going to the groomer. As soon as he realizes where we are, he drops down on the floor like a dog that melted, forcing me to drag him across the polished concrete. And then there's that moment after the groomer picks him up, right before she

103

disappears into the back room, when Pip pops his little head over her shoulder and gives me one long, last, Pound Puppy look.

My heart hurts just thinking about it.

Last spring, I picked him up after a grooming and noticed right away that he could not stop blinking. They assured me it was likely stray cut hairs irritating his eyes, that's all. But by the evening, he couldn't even open his eyes. I took him to the vet the next morning, and he was diagnosed with corneal abrasions in both eyes, likely from contact with a chemical. His puppy-dog eyes would need antibiotic ointment applied twice daily for a week to heal.

I felt terrible. How had I let this happen to my baby?

You might be surprised to know that I was nice when I called the grooming-shop manager. I said I knew it was an accident, but I was "disappointed" that my dog got hurt.

I holstered the Philly inside me.

And they were very apologetic and promised to reimburse me for the vet bill. We hung up on good terms.

But this should go without saying — they're dead to me.

I'm Mother Mary's granddaughter. Pip is Mother Mary's great-granddog.

We forgive.

We never forget.

So this summer, I had to look into other options for his summer cut. And after scouring countless reviews of groomers all over the city, in the end the answer was clear.

The only person I trust to clip this dog is me.

I have a defiant streak. I often imagine I would be good at things I've never tried before.

I think the Latin for that is *hubris.*

I must get this from my mother, who had similar delusions about her hairdressing abilities and cut my hair until I was five.

My bangs as a kid were Bettie Page-short and Lawnmower Man-uneven.

But nobody sprayed a chemical in my eyes.

And for me, there's a divine justice to screwing up on your own, and a frustration when you pay someone else to do it. I genuinely feel at peace if I try my best and fail.

On the other hand, I self-berate endlessly when someone else messes up for me. I blame myself for not communicating clearly enough, or supervising them properly, or choosing the right person to hire, or for not saying something sooner, and on and on it goes. The less control I have, the more I blame myself.

I realize now that this is illogical. I should probably see a therapist.

But instead, I watched dog-grooming instructional videos online and fired up the Wahl clipper.

Step one: wash and completely blow-dry your dog. This will make the clipper move cleanly, evenly, and safely through the dog's fur.

Washing Pip is always fun. He's placid in the water, but as soon as I towel him off, he becomes turbocharged and zooms all over my apartment, rubbing himself on all the furniture.

Once he's tuckered out, he alternates between sitting in front of the blow-dryer with the poise of a Beyoncé video, and getting sick of it and running away while I chase him with it like a ray gun.

Finally, an hour later, he was soft and fluffy as a cloud. But I wasn't done. I hadn't even started.

Step two: clip your dog. Okay, I can do this. But where? I obviously don't have a professional grooming table, and doing it on any eating surface seemed like a bad idea.

"Well, you can't do it in the apartment!" my mom said over the phone. "You have to do it outside."

This is the perspective of someone who does not live on an island of 8 million people.

I explained to her that my neighbors would not appreciate me camping out on the sidewalk and sending one million fur tumbleweeds down a busy city street.

I figured if I laid a towel down on the living-room floor, most of the hair would stay there, right? It's not like there's a gust of wind indoors.

By the end of our grooming session, my apartment looked like a shaken snow globe of white dog fur.

And the end took *forever* to get to.

The YouTube groomer said it should take about fifteen to twenty minutes to clip a Shih Tzu's entire body.

My question is, are you Shih-Tzu'ing me?

With him wriggling around, me missing spots, giving him breaks, giving him bribes, carefully scissor-cutting his face, and trying to keep remotely on top of the copious amounts of hair flying all over my apartment, it took me *three hours* to clip Pip's entire body.

I was so exhausted, I left his paws to do the next day, so he had a teddy bear body with Dr. Seuss floofy feet.

I was exhausted, but happy. I know I'm biased, but to me, he looked perfect.

Because in spite of the paws and some uneven patches here and there, Pip looked like the dog I loved more than anything in the world.

And by that wagging tail, I knew he felt like it, too.

Before

During

After

My Thoughts, Crystallized

LISA

I just got back from a vacation in Sedona, Arizona.

Woo-hoo!

Or should I say, woo-woo?

Let me explain.

I got the idea for this vacation because Francesca always wanted to see the Grand Canyon, but I can't say I was yearning to see it. I thought, look at a picture and you get the idea.

Or so I thought.

It was only the first thing I was wrong about on our vacation.

Because it turns out that the Grand Canyon is even more grand than you think, though it is still terrifying to someone who has vertigo, even when viewed from the snack bar.

But that's not the point of this column.

Or of this journey, or even of Sedona.

I can't remember where I heard about

111

Sedona, except that I heard it had energy vortexes, which were supposed to be natural formations in the red rocks that produced magnetic fields or something like that.

I'm no scientist.

I'm just a suburban lady who feels tired, like every suburban lady in the world, or at least in the suburbs.

Bottom line, the energy vortex sounded like a good thing. I did my research and it turned out there were six or seven energy vortexes in the Sedona area, and I started to get excited about the idea of going there and getting seven times the energy.

Like a vacation that recharges you, literally.

Which appealed to me because I'm Type A and I'm writing three books a year. I figured if I went to seven energy vortexes, I could rack up seven times the energy, and write twenty-one books a year, if I'm doing my multiplication correctly.

In other words, I could go from Type A to Type A+++++++.

I could raise my grade in life and even go for extra credit.

I could make more money on less caffeination.

I would have vortex power!

You get the idea.

Plus I would undoubtedly have extra energy to come home, clean out my closet, file my bills, and throw away my old bras, which is every bra I own.

I think I took French II in my favorite bra.

In fact, I still own the bra I took the SATs in, though the cups must not have been the same size, since my English score was high and my math score couldn't fill a demi-cup.

The only problem was that Francesca and I couldn't drive anywhere when we went to Sedona, mainly because I'm too scared to drive at heights, so we hired a guide who took us on the energy vortex tour. The brochure said that the guide knew a lot about geology, vortexes, and Indian culture, and was even a medicine man.

My only thought was, Is he single?

A medicine man is kind of like a doctor.

Or at least he qualifies, to me.

But of course it turns out that he has a girlfriend.

I didn't ask if she was a medicine woman.

Anyway, as it turned out, our guide was very nice and very smart, and when he takes us to the first energy vortex, he's honest enough to tell us that he's not sure that he believes in the energy vortex thing at all.

Francesca was fine with it, but I was aghast. I wanted my energy back. Or failing that, my money.

But I didn't say any of that because it would've sounded crass and materialistic, and I was already getting the idea that Sedona is definitely one of the more Zen places on the earth.

Lisa and Francesca get reenergized!

Which I thought would be a dumb thing, but as it turns out, is a great thing.

So our guide took us to one of the highest points in the canyon that was previously known as an energy vortex, and he set up a medicine wheel, which for you medicine-wheel virgins like me, means that you basically put four rocks in a circle, stand in front of the rock, and think about your life.

I was still grumbling to myself when we stood there in stillness, and my brain was thinking about a million things, basically calculating how much energy I was losing by the second, like I was a human battery and the level was inching into the red zone.

But Francesca stayed nice and still, and so did the guide, and so did I, since I didn't want to flunk medicine wheel.

I wanted an A+!

And in time I began to contemplate the beauty of the surroundings, the rich redness of the rocks, and the clear azure of the sky, and then I listened to the stillness of the wind whispering through the canyon, and I watched a hawk soaring overhead, gliding on currents I couldn't see.

And I stopped wanting my money back.

I felt recharged, as if my spiritual phone had been plugged in all night long.

The journey turned out to be a spiritual one, after all.

Later I even bought crystals, books on Zen Buddhism, and three strings of prayer flags, which I hung all over the house when I got home.

I'm hoping they'll remind me that the

energy is in me, not in any vortex.

And if I forget, there's always caffeine.

LISA NAPPOLINE

LISA

I don't have many talents, but I have one I wish I could use more.

I can take a nap anywhere, at any time.

Even now.

I just woke up. I'm not even kidding.

It's a gray afternoon and too cold for May, and I started to feel drowsy and relaxed.

I knew exactly what I needed.

Bradley Cooper.

Sorry not sorry.

Kidding not kidding.

I needed Bradley Cooper, but what I got was a nap.

I stretched out with the dogs on the couch and pretty soon we were all asleep, pretending we don't have to work for a living.

I love naps.

And I'm good at them.

Yet I know somebody who says she can't nap at all. She tries and tries but she can't take a nap.

Which makes me wonder.

About myself.

I wonder why she can't nap and I can, so easily.

In fact, I can barely stay awake.

Maybe she's smarter, or more ambitious, or more important, and her mind is busier than mine, buzzing with big thoughts, formulating things-to-do, solving equations, and answering email.

Not me.

I got nothing.

Remember Curly in *The Three Stooges*? He said, "I'm trying to think, but nothing happens."

That's me.

Nyuk nyuk.

But my friend who can't nap is not alone. Evidently, a lot of people can't nap, so much so that there is actually a class for napping.

Did you hear about this?

It's a class that you can take with forty-five other adults, and the instructor will teach you how to take a nap. The class is called Napercize because they stretch before they take their nap.

This would be my kind of cardio.

I would do great in that class.

Also in Eatercize.

I would *crush* in Eatercize.

But can you imagine taking a nap with forty-five strangers?

I would rather nap with forty-five dogs.

Because dogs, you can trust.

Once I took a nap on a plane, and while I was asleep, the guy next to me got a blanket and covered me.

Dude, no.

But I'm not sure you can teach napping. I think it's in the DNA. Some families pass on math abilities, but The Flying Scottolines are congenitally sleepy.

Every night, Mother Mary took a nap on

Lisa learned to nap from the queen of napping, Mother Mary!

the couch and my father took a nap on the floor.

It was a great marriage until they both woke up.

Brother Frank can nap like a champ, and Daughter Francesca has inherited these valuable genes. Sometimes when she comes home, we eat lunch and then take a nap on the couch. We wake up and stretch like kittens, just in time for dinner and another nap.

I know, you think we're depressed.

But we're not.

We're relaxed.

When Francesca and I went on book tour last July, we would have two signings a day, one at noon and one at night, but in between, we would park the car somewhere and take a nap.

There's no nap like a car nap.

Extra points if you sleep with your mouth open.

Double extra points if you drool.

Drooling is proof of an awesome nap.

When I wake up from a nap with the dogs, I drool more than they do.

I mean, the couch is soaked.

The only problem is that the world has changed around The Slumbering Scottolines.

Nobody takes naps anymore.

People are running around like crazy, checking their phones and increasing their productivity.

Plus if you close your eyes these days, you'll miss something, especially with so much political news. I took a few naps recently, and every time I woke up, somebody had gotten fired.

I think my napping is causing national unemployment.

So I promise to stay awake.

For as long as I can.

But now I gotta go.

It's time for Cakercise.

City Slickers 3: The Legend of Bandana-Napkin

FRANCESCA

They say you don't really know a person until you travel together, but is that true if the person is your mother?

I asked myself this on our recent trip to Arizona, our first mother-daughter vacation in almost ten years. We had an amazing time and got along great, but I noticed some new quirks, beginning as soon as our first flight.

"Can you open the window?" she asked.

"Sure." I slid the shade up and squinted into the light. "Wow, you can see —"

"Nm-mm," my mother grunted, and I noticed she was shielding her eyes.

"Sorry, too bright?"

"No, I don't want to see how high we are, it scares me."

Now I squinted at her. "You asked me to open it."

"Yes, but I don't want to *see*!"

I know her, but do I understand her?

I wondered again by the pool in Scottsdale, when I lowered my sunglasses to see my mother approaching with what appeared to be a cloth napkin tied around her head.

"Perfect, huh?" She posed like a pirate beauty queen. "I went to the gift shop for something to cover my head, but then I realized, I could get this from the restaurant! It's just like a bandana!"

"It's even more like a napkin." And I reminded her she had a ball cap in the bag.

"Nah, the brim blocks the sun." She settled down on the chair next to me, readjusting her bandana-napkin.

I slid down behind my book.

Another of my mom's quirks is that she loves to order drinks, or "dwinks" when she's ready to party, but she hates the taste of straight alcohol. She always forgets this last part.

"Can I taste it?" She sipped my dry Sauvignon Blanc and grimaced. "So *winey.*"

She prefers fruity cocktails. One of the only wines sweet enough for her is Lambrusco, an unusual, sparkling red, and when she asks for it, she tricks waiters into thinking she's a jaded oenophile. Most restaurants don't have it, so the waiter will suggest other esoteric options, using words like "tannic" and "peaty."

I wanted to tell him, she wants notes of

"juice box," do you have a juice box wine?

As the server left to bring a sample of a "jammy" Pinot Noir I knew she'd suffer through, I said, "You don't have to order a drink."

"Of course I do, we're on vacation!"

She had a point.

I was getting the hang of Vacation Mom, when I anticipated a problem. If a peek out an airplane window was too much for her vertigo, how was she going to enjoy the Grand Canyon?

The irony was that she'd planned the trip. The Grand Canyon was entirely her idea; she had even booked a guide to take us hiking into it.

I sat her down. "I'm worried about you. You need to mentally prep that it's going to be really, really huge and you might get freaked out by the height."

She waved me off. "It'll be great, I just won't go on the high parts."

"Mom, I think the whole thing is a high part."

Cue the soundtrack to *City Slickers.*

But when the day came, my mom closed her eyes for much of the mountainous drive up (don't worry, she was in the backseat) yet remained in good spirits!

We arrived at the Canyon, and the guide

It took us all day to work up to getting my mom this close to the edge for this photo, and I'm very proud of her!

showed us to the top of the steep trail. Or at least he pointed to it from a safe distance since my mom refused to get out of the car. I said I couldn't leave her in there like a dog, but she insisted:

"You go, that's why I hired him, I want you to have a good time."

I was touched. And I realized how much of my mom's behavior was to make me happy: a good view from the window seat, fun drinks at dinner — okay, the napkin thing was just weird, I got nothing for that

— but she wouldn't let her quirks keep us from having an unforgettable vacation.

In the end, I made it less than thirty minutes down into the Canyon before my own vertigo forced me to turn back. When I reemerged on the top, flat ground, there was no sweeter sight than my little mom, bravely out of the car, trying to take a photo with a shaky hand while gripping onto a signpost for dear life — a good ten yards from the gorge's edge.

When she saw me, she broke into a grin, still clinging to the signpost like a koala. "How was it?"

I smiled. "Perfect."

THE ANSWER IS BLOWING IN THE WIND CHIMES

LISA

The world divides into people who own wind chimes, and the rest of us.

But now I'm crossing over.

I say this because I was still in my Sedona-induced haze when I came home, and I found a new appreciation for a small set of wind chimes that a reader was kind enough to give me.

Yes, readers give me presents. How great is that?

But no, you don't have to. You're reading one of my books, that's present enough and I may come over and give you a hug. And if you bought the book, I'll force my tongue down your throat.

But in a good way.

Just kidding.

Anyway, in my New Age middle age, I have developed an appreciation for crystals, yoga, and yes, wind chimes.

I hung the small set in my backyard and

forgot about them. I never really noticed the sound they made, though I work in the room nearest them. The only sounds I heard were the tapping of my keyboard, the TV in the background, and the snoring of five dogs.

In other words, music.

You're my kind of person if the sound-track of your life includes dog farts.

But the other day, the dogs were outside, the TV was off, and for a minute, I stopped working. The window was open, and the sweet sounds of the wind chimes wafted through the screen, like a twinkly breeze.

I know. I've lost my damn mind. Can dreamcatchers be far behind?

And I started really appreciating the sound of the chimes, then waiting for the next breeze so I could hear them chime again.

This would not be a path to career success.

Bottom line, I fell in love with wind chimes.

But as in typical Type A fashion, as much as I liked the wind chimes in my backyard, I started to think I needed a pair of wind chimes for the front yard. And maybe also for the side yard. And maybe outside my bedroom window. Because if some is good, more is better, and there is no such thing as excess when it comes to woo-woo.

Or junk you can hang on a tree.

Anyway, I found myself online looking up wind chimes. It's not exactly spiritual to buy wind chimes from Amazon, but they offer several hundred nice ones, and then I found a bunch of wind-chime stores online that had four basic types, namely Bamboo, Capiz, "Fun," and Traditional.

I clicked through to Traditional since I don't know what Capiz is and I'm not "fun."

And in Traditional, they actually let you listen to the chimes.

Bring your own wind.

I got plenty.

So do my dogs.

To stay on point, to hear the chimes, all you do is click the button that says LISTEN TO ME.

What woman doesn't want a button like that?

Or one that says, DO WHAT I SAY WHEN I SAY IT.

Or PASS THE CHOCOLATE CAKE.

But I digress.

When you click the button, the wind chimes play actual songs.

Wait. What?

Who knew that wind chimes played anything but random notes?

What a country!

And as for what the chimes played, we're not talking "Mary Had a Little Lamb." For example, there's an Amazing Grace chime that plays "Amazing Grace."

Amazing!

And a Spanish Garden chime that, according to the website, plays the "opening minor chord of the *adagio* movement from the *Concerto de Aranjuez* by Joaquín Rodrigo, one of the most significant Spanish composers of the twentieth century."

Olé!

So I spent an hour listening to all the chimes and trying to pick one, which was like choosing a ringtone for your tree.

They were all so different, like Bells of Paradise (tinkly), Chakra Chime (metaphysical), Fantasy Fairy (magical), and Hummingbird (caffeinated). There were even chimes from different places, like Ireland, Kyoto, Jerusalem, and Patagonia, which I think is near Camden.

But pretty soon all of the chimes started sounding like each other, and I couldn't remember which chime sounded like what and my nerves started to fray. I didn't know which song, spirit animal, religion, or nationality I wanted my wind chimes to be.

Or maybe that should be up to the wind chimes themselves.

Who am I to decide?

The answer, my friend, is blowing in the wind chimes.

Everything's Coming up Roses

LISA

It's that time of year again.

When my garden blooms, despite my best efforts to the contrary.

I can't take any credit.

The answer is perennials.

Every spring, they come back all by themselves, and I don't have to do anything.

Even flowers that I thought I killed came back, which is my kind of plant.

They're not only dummyproof, they're bulletproof.

Anyway, blooming in my garden right now are peonies, primrose, and a purple flower that I forget the name of.

Welcome to gardening for the middle-aged, where you can't remember what you planted.

I did make a map of the garden, but I can't remember where I put it.

So now, every day there's a new flower that blooms, utterly to my surprise. It's like

I wrote a book that I don't remember the ending to, which also happens.

Impressed yet?

But the big news is that I'm about to expand the garden, because, of course, it turns out that gardening is just like every other form of home improvement — if you paint one wall, you end up building an addition.

Wait, what?

Let me explain.

The garden is in front of my house but I couldn't see it from the kitchen because there was a wall in the way, so then I opened the kitchen and added a little room that overlooks the garden, and it's finally finished and it's glorious.

I'm spending my retirement savings, but if you keep reading, I'll keep writing.

Until 2084.

Also I put in a white picket fence around the front yard so I could work in the garden with the dogs, instead of having to lock them in the house. Which is where our story begins, because I started taking a second look at the white picket fence and picturing it with some beautiful flowers in front, or maybe flowers that would climb the fence, which actually has a trellis over the gate.

You know where this is going if you've

The garden that inspired a new garden room!

read fairy tales, watched *Downton Abbey,* or have estrogen.

A trellis begs for some kind of climbing vine or flower, so I read a bunch of books on flowers and tried to pick something that could grow on the fence and trellis.

But I kept coming back to the same flower. Roses.

I love roses. They smell incredible and they're beautiful.

Plus I've never grown them successfully before. I have two rosebushes now, but one gets black spot, the other gets white spot, and they both get Japanese beetles.

So I struck out twice, but that's never stopped me before.

Maybe they're just the Thing One and Thing Two of roses.

You don't give up on marriage just because you got the wrong rosebush.

If you follow.

And the more rose books I read, the more I learned that there were hundreds of varieties with fancy names like Lady Sylvia, Madame Gregoire Staechelin, and Reine Marie Henriette, which felt girlpowery and pretentious.

Me, in a nutshell.

And roses come in so many different colors like crimson reds, creamy whites, buttery yellows, and the palest of pinks, but then I found a rose that was my favorite color:

Hot Pink.

Or at my age, Hot Flash Pink.

The name of the rose was Zephirine Drouhin, which is supposed to be very fragrant and completely thornless, which *also* describes me in a nutshell.

So I settled on the Zephirine Drouhin, measured the fence line, and counted that I need twenty-five rosebushes to cover the fence and the trellis.

Um, that's a lot.

I'm going all in on something I've never grown before.
And I'm spending money.
But did that stop me?
Are you new around here?
I just ordered the rosebushes.
You know what this means.
Everything's coming up Retirement Fund.

I DABBLE

FRANCESCA

How old is too old to paint a picture for your mother?

I have a new hobby: watercolors.

I picked it up while we were in Arizona. When I saw our Sedona resort offered a watercolor class, I signed us up before they showed us the room.

My mom teased me. "It's gonna be all little kids."

Actually, it was mostly women her age and older, but no matter. By the first stroke of color, I was smitten.

Love at first splat.

Back home, I'd barely unpacked before I went to buy my supplies.

New hobbies are a great excuse to go shopping.

But it's been awhile since I was a rank beginner at anything. The first time I went to the store, I was so intimidated by the potential presence of *real artists,* I researched my shopping list in advance and didn't talk to a soul.

Of course I got half the wrong stuff.

When I went back the second time, the cool-haircut-quotient among the patrons remained high, but no one noticeably judged me as a dilettante. No one was looking at me at all.

Serious artists are so focused.

This time, I sought advice, I asked dumb questions, I had much more fun.

People are nice to beginners, especially if you're beginning at something they love. The salesman there was also a watercolorist, and he led me around like a puppy, even saving me from buying several items I didn't need.

I didn't clarify: "I'm not a starving artist, I'm just always on a diet."

For less than a hundred bucks (far less if I'd asked for help the first time), I'm all set up.

And I absolutely love it. I paint mostly at night and mostly of Pip, but I'm expanding into other flora and fauna. It's so fun and engrossing. It's the one activity during which I can't multitask.

I have to strike while the water is wet.

Afterwards, I feel as refreshed and centered as I do after yoga, but I didn't have to

My very first watercolor of my favorite subject: Pip! My muse is the cutest.

hold in my farts.

I also think watercolors are fixing my brain.

(Although I did accidentally take a sip from my mug of brush-water, so it might be the cadmium.)

Like most of my friends, I thought I had no time for a hobby. Yet somehow I found time to check Facebook, Twitter, and Instagram twenty times a day.

My brain has gotten really good at scanning, refreshing, multitasking, and generally behaving like a toddler on Pixy Stix.

We need to slow our brains down, stretch those attention spans beyond 140 characters, and rebuild the muscles of concentration. Now, when I hear some political news that would normally send me rage-scrolling Twitter, I can paint pretty flowers instead.

For the first time, I feel more recharged than my phone.

Sure, I haven't entirely replaced social media. I started following a lot of #watercolor accounts for inspiration and tutorials.

More accurately, I'm following #акварель

For my mom's birthday, I painted her favorite childhood photo of me.

A watercolor of a bird, shown before I messed up the background

because it seems that as much as they love fur hats and sad novels, Russians love watercolors.

They must start painting with borscht as children, because every amazing watercolor artist I found on Instagram is in Moscow.

Either that or they hacked the algorithm.

But whether I'm following #FakeArt or not, my feed is so much more soothing now. Watching a video of someone paint peonies is much better than skimming filtered photos of better bodies, better vacations, and better brunch.

And I did share a picture of my first watercolor painting, a little Pip portrait, on my account. The encouragement from my friends felt great, my painting got far more hearts than my selfies, but I didn't do it for the likes.

I felt proud of my artwork, and I wanted to share it with my new friends Ekaterina and Ludmila.

My generation is obsessed with life-hacks and #fitspo, living life harder, better, faster, stronger. The message is free time should be spent on physical self-improvement or maximizing efficiency, something to make you more datable, employable, or enviable.

Can we carve out time for fun?

I'm into watercolors, but I have some cool girlfriends who knit, and who knows? Elaborate train sets could be the next hipster-dude craze.

I'd take it over the lumberjack beards any day.

So that's my millennial argument for old-fashioned hobbies.

Do something today that makes you happy without a filter.

And I hope my mom likes her painting.

Not-So-Kiddie Table
LISA

I don't know when this happened, but it did.

I'm officially one of the old people at the wedding.

You know, one of the "parents' friends."

I used to roll my eyes at those people.

I used to begrudge them seats at the wedding.

I thought they were taking up room for my friends.

And now I am them.

So there is justice in the world.

I realized it this weekend, when I went to a wonderful wedding. I knew the terrific young woman who got married, and I watched her grow up. She used to be the horse-crazy daughter of one of my dear friends, and she became a large-animal veterinarian, so she's still horse-crazy, by profession.

Smart girl.

The bride's sister was the same way, and I remember her growing up too, running around in pigtails and paddock boots, eating potato chips out of a bag. She grew up to be a doctor, so she's a smart girl, too.

I was delighted that their mother asked Francesca and me to the wedding, and we enjoyed the ceremony together, sitting with a lot of other mothers and daughters. But we parted ways at the reception, when the daughters went to sit at the young-people table and the mothers went elsewhere.

You guessed it, the old-people table.

This is remarkable, since it seems like only yesterday that I was at the kiddie table.

Do you remember the kiddie table?

The Flying Scottolines were big on the kiddie table. Mostly because, as you may recall, Mother Mary was the youngest of nineteen children.

Nineteen is a lot of kiddies.

Now imagine that those kiddies grow up and have a lot of kiddies themselves, and you're basically looking at a sea of kiddie tables at our house, every Sunday when I was growing up.

They all came over for Sunday dinner, which was always spaghetti and meatballs.

I'm not sure why everyone came to our house as opposed to anyone else's, but

Mother Mary would want me to tell you that it was because she made the best gravy.

Which is South Philly for tomato sauce.

So at my house, it wasn't a question of whether you sat at the kiddie table, it was a question of which kiddie table you're going to sit at. There were card tables everywhere you looked, and a lot of kids slurping spaghetti with a napkin tucked in their collars.

Same with the adults.

I still do that, myself.

Even in restaurants.

By the way, in our family, the kids at the kiddie table ate the same food as the adults. I've heard that this wasn't true in other families, where the adults got the good stuff and the kids got fish sticks.

Come to think of it, fish sticks are pretty great.

But in our family, we all ate the same thing, and we also ate the same thing every night, as we lacked imagination, food-wise.

When dinner was over, the kids left the house and went outside to play, which is something that children did in the olden days.

When did my life become a history lesson?

Anyway, after I grew out of the kiddie

table, I had two weddings and two divorces, and then I blinked my eyes and the weddings were of my friends' children, and that's how, last weekend, I ended up at the old-people table.

I realized it because the first thing I noticed at the table was the centerpiece, which was a lovely runner of fresh wildflowers. All of us olds noticed it too, and pretty soon we were talking about the centerpiece, and that was when it struck me that I had never cared about centerpieces before.

This is a side effect of menopause.

A Centerpiece Obsession.

In fact, I remember in the past, I would go to weddings and see women at the table fight over the centerpiece or go through the polite minuet of "you take it," "no, *you* take it," which is the reverse-fighting-over-it way of women.

Either way, I would think that was really crazy.

I would think, *Lady, buy your own damn flowers.*

But now I want the centerpiece.

And I've been known to fight over the centerpiece.

And if someone says to me, "No, *you* take it," guess what I do.

I take it!

And so, in the end, the old-people table suits me just fine.

And the good news is, we olds had a great time at the wedding.

Start with the fact that we're still alive.

And the fact that we love to dance, and so we did, with each other and with our daughters, with the bride and her sister, and her friends, and the groom's friends and family, which is what weddings are about, after all.

Like life itself.

All of us, together.

From kiddie table, onward.

Dancing.

LOVE BOAT

LISA

It's everybody's favorite time of year again.

My birthday!

That's how I feel about my birthday, and that's how I feel about yours, too.

I celebrate your birthday in my head, so I hope you're celebrating mine in your head.

It's cheaper that way.

Also we don't get drunk.

Well, maybe I do.

But this birthday felt different to me, in a good way.

I feel superhappy just to be alive.

Let's pause a moment.

I know that sounds kind of Splenda, but it's really true. And the fact is, absolutely nothing has changed from last year.

In fact that's exactly what is making me happy.

It really is a good thing to be grateful sometimes that you're still living.

I get constant reminders of this, and I had

one just this weekend, with Francesca. We were scheduled to give a speech about the previous book in this series, entitled *I Need a Lifeguard Everywhere but the Pool.*

Actually I need a lifeguard at the pool, too.

But that's another story.

Literally.

Anyway, we were supposed to speak at the American Library Association conference in Chicago, and we were both excited because we love librarians.

Hug your librarian the next time you see him or her.

They don't get enough hugs.

Nobody does.

See what I mean?

Splenda!

Anyway, when I go on a business trip, I fly out, do my gig, and fly right back. I don't do anything other than the gig, because it's business.

But Francesca had a different idea. "Mom, I've never been to Chicago," she said. "Why don't we go sightseeing and leave later that night?"

I rolled my eyes. Inwardly.

Don't roll your eyes outwardly if you're a mother.

You'll get in a lot of trouble.

But I said yes, and Francesca went online, researching the things you could do in Chicago, which I heard about with an inward eyeroll.

Because I didn't think you were supposed to have fun on a business trip.

And before I knew it, we were in Chicago, we did our gig, talked about our book, and gave a lot of hugs, then we woke up the next day, ready for tourist fun in the sun.

What did we do?

We saw the cool bean statue at Millennium Park.

Cool beans!

And we went to the gorgeous Buckingham Fountain, which is next to a body of water they say is a lake but anybody from Philly would call an ocean.

But the best thing we did was take a boat ride with a billion other tourists down the Chicago River, with a volunteer telling us the architectural history of the skyscrapers.

Inward eyeroll?

Same here, but I was wrong.

It was awesome.

Because this amazing volunteer knew everything about architecture and gave us almost two hours of her time simply because she loves architecture and her city.

And because we learned everything about

the brilliant architects and engineers who imagined and then built a slew of incredible buildings, each of them a tribute to human ingenuity and hard work.

And even because people on the bank waved to our boat as we floated by, and Francesca and I waved back, even though we had no idea who they were, or they us.

In fact, we waved at people on the riverbanks the whole damn boat trip, and people on the riverbanks waved back, and that made Francesca and me tear up, unaccountably.

Okay, accountably, since we're Italian-American.

We cry all the time.

That's how you know we're happy.

The boat trip was a reminder of the simple truth that we're all just human beings, floating down some river, waving at each other as we go by.

And when I thought of the architects, the engineers, the volunteers, and the librarians, I felt awed by all of us, just normal people, filled with so much vision and heart, following whichever endeavor we choose, our passion or our job and sometimes both. With just ourselves, we build communities, cities, and even countries.

Like this one.

And by the end of the day, I remembered I was happy to be alive.

You probably already know this lesson, but in my life, I need to teach it to myself from time to time.

Which is to go slower.

Enjoy yourself.

Feel the sun on your face.

Wave.

And do really touristy things, because there's a reason so many people like to do the same things, wherever they go.

Because people are basically the same, everywhere you go.

Happy tourists!

We're all tourists in this life, aren't we?
None of us is from here.
And none of us is staying.
And so my biggest birthday present was that I got another year on my trip.
I pray that will be your present, too.
Happy birthday to us.

The Live Feed Must Go On

FRANCESCA

Have you ever tried helping your parent learn a new technology?

Now, imagine doing so while being filmed live.

That's what I had to do a few weeks ago when our publisher wanted my mom and me to record our first Facebook Live event.

Facebook Live is when you record and post a live video, during which viewers can post questions and comments for you to respond to in real time.

"So someone will write the questions on cue cards for us?" my mom asked.

I patiently explained that no, the questions would be coming too fast, so we would have to read the comments in real time.

"But then I'd need my reading glasses," she said, getting to the heart of the matter, "and I won't look pretty on the video."

I told her I would read the questions, and we decided to host the chat while we were recording our audiobook for our previous essay collection, *I Need a Lifeguard Everywhere but the Pool.*

For those who may not know, we record our audiobooks ourselves, so you can hear what my mom calls, "our authentic Philly accents."

I understand mad and sad should rhyme, but in my mouth, they don't.

Our publisher kindly sent a social-media whiz to help us. She was armed only with an iPad and an LED light, instead of the cookies and squeaky toy required to keep us focused.

We thought it would be cool to film in the recording studio, but it didn't turn out that way. When we recorded our audiobook, we stood in front of a screen draped with a heavy Turkish rug for extra acoustic softening. So when we first set up the shot, we looked like we were coming to you live from Istanbul Public Access Television.

So we arranged ourselves against a different wall, but the lighting wasn't as good on that side. Lighting is delicate for Italian-Americans like us. Our noses require diffused light, lest we become human sundials.

We really needed the Mariah Carey soft-halo lighting, but what we had to work with was a twelve-inch stick light on an alligator clamp.

And we couldn't have it in the shot, so it couldn't be in front of us. Instead, we clipped it to a music stand off to the side. But then we looked like we were coming to you live from the path of an oncoming train.

Thankfully, our social-media maven came to our rescue and MacGyvered the light in the best possible position. She gave us the countdown and we started the live video.

For the first seven minutes, we got a handful of hellos and several questions that we happily answered.

That was the author version of Seven Minutes in Heaven, because after that, nothing.

Even crickets would've been preferable. At least they chirp.

The social-media equivalent of crickets is a sad little tally of a dozen likes and fewer comments.

I kept trying to low-key refresh the scroll to see if any new comments had arrived, but they hadn't. My mom was doing the same, but she got confused on which direction to scroll and kept going back to the early ones and accidentally shut down the video window completely.

We were filming a live Facebook chat with

no one to chat with.

Luckily, talking is kind of our thing. We've had thirty-one years of practice yapping to each other, maintained with a healthy diet of one-to-three phone calls a day.

What we filmed is basically our relationship in its purest form, interrupting each other and laughing about whatever pops into our heads.

Fun!

Back home, we logged on to watch our video, mostly to judge the nose shadows, and we were shocked to see loads of questions that were asked live but hadn't gotten through to us.

Our feed must have frozen. We'd thought the worst thing about video-recording in a sound booth was the lighting — the real problem was the Wi-Fi.

The good news is, the live video transmitted to viewers perfectly. You can view the recording on our Facebook pages now. But I still feel terrible if some of you thought we were ignoring your questions.

I promise, it was accidental. Believe me, we would've loved to include everyone in the conversation.

That would've been our dream come true.

All of us, interrupting each other, together.

DRESSY

LISA

Guess what I got for my birthday?

A dress with a bra already sewn into it.

You didn't know that was a thing?

Or rather, two things?

I didn't either.

But my bestie Franca did, and not only do I thank her for the dress, but I got this story out of it, which is awesome.

To explain, I've seen tank tops that are for yoga, which have a bra sewn in, and that I understand. But I'm talking about a flowery cotton shift that was otherwise normal except for two massive foamy cups, sewn into the front of the dress.

I packed the dress for book tour, not realizing there was a bra inside until I tried it on in the hotel room, then looked at myself in the mirror.

D'oh.

The dress fit great except that the foam cups were way bigger than my breasts, which are your basic B.

For Boobs.

The cups were like a C or maybe even a D, which is a terrible grade in anything but mammaries.

I don't know who wears these bra dresses.

Strippers who love florals.

So you get the idea.

My cups were half-empty.

Or half-full, for you optimists.

Either way, they gave my chest a pair of dimples far lower than they're supposed to be.

Plus the pads were higher than my breasts, so I had double-decker nipples, which is not a good look even on dogs.

Evidently, the world thinks our breasts should be earrings.

I didn't get it. Then I realized that maybe the dress wasn't for my age group. It was a size eight, not size sixty-two.

But I hadn't packed another dress for the book signing.

What's an author to do?

I took off the dress and examined the seams to see if I could take the pads out, but I couldn't. I put the dress back on and tried to figure out what to do with my breasts. I pushed them up into the cups, but they wouldn't stay there because there was nothing to hold them up, like elastic or an underwire.

Or a suspension cable.

Or a crane.

Gravity is real, people.

I took the dress off again, put on a bra, and put the dress back on. Of course the only bra I had with me was my good bra, since that's what I save for book tour.

Every woman has a good bra.

You know it's the good bra because it's new and cost too much.

"New" means bought less than five years ago. If you have mustard older than your bra, your bra is new.

Also a good bra has lace, because women think men care about lace.

When they have boobs in front of their face.

Guess again.

Or the good bra is a sexy color, like red.

For harlots.

Or black.

For harlots with class.

I go with black.

I have aspriations.

And my good bra is padded because my breasts want to sell a lot of books.

They want to be breast-sellers.

Sorry.

So back to the story, I put my bra and the dress on, which meant I was wearing a padded bra with a padded-bra dress.

You're thinking I looked bad?

On the contrary.

I looked great!

Okay, I had a bad case of boob sweat, but you have to look for the silver lining.

In the dress lining.

I would sell tons of books if my audience were composed mostly of men or the blind.

Because you could be blind and still see my chest, which had turned into The Continental Shelf.

I mean, you could use my chest as a bookcase.

Or a bar, if you want to rest a beer and a bowl of chips.

I turned to look at myself, and my breasts were sticking out so far they bumped into the wall.

Luckily I felt nothing.

I bounced back.

It was like wearing a trampoline.

I feel pretty sure I would be a flotation device.

Or a bulletproof vest.

In any event, I wore the dress and I sold plenty of books, so my grades improved from D to A+ .

And here is my question:

Why stop at bras?

If we're going to start sewing underwear into dresses, why not sew in a pair of panties, too?

Then you could just jump in from above and be ready for the day.

Like Supergirl, with implants.

SEEDY

LISA

I've succumbed to the siren song.

Of prepared foods.

Don't tell Mother Mary.

I don't know why this happened to me, but it did. Maybe because in summertime I find myself in the grocery store a million times a week, yet I never know what to make for dinner.

And then I happen to pass a counter that had dinner made for me.

Corn was shucked, carrots were chopped into perfect circles, and zucchini was spiralized.

That's a verb I didn't even know until I saw spiralized zucchini glistening in the display case, where all of the foods were taken out of their natural containers, chopped, diced, sliced, and wrapped in plastic, already prepared for me.

I used to think this was a bad thing.

But times change.

And now I'm addicted.

I don't even know how to cut anything anymore.

I'm throwing away all my knives.

And spiralizers.

I don't own one of those, but I'm going to buy one and throw it right out.

If you had told me that I would buy Brussels sprouts simply because someone else had already cut them in half for me, I would have thought you were crazy.

But now I'm the crazy one.

They even have cauliflower minced into such tiny bits that it looks like rice, so they're now changing vegetables into grains and probably back again.

It's gotten out of control, but I'm not complaining.

All I do is pick up the plastic packet, drizzle the stuff with olive oil, and throw it in the oven.

I know, it sounds like a great dinner for about a week, but then what started happening was that I was getting even too lazy for the foods that you had to drizzle with anything and throw in anything else, so I found myself sidling over to the prepared-foods case, which are displayed in hot or refrigerated bins, depending on your mood.

Or temperature.

What a country!

So instead of buying groceries in the grocery store, I was buying complete meals, already-made Caesar salads, vegetarian dumplings, and even sushi.

You haven't lived until you've had grocery-store sushi.

Then I noticed my sushi section has something called power lunch, which is a salad with green beans, red and yellow peppers, quinoa, and Tataki salmon.

I don't know what Tataki means.

I'm guessing overpriced.

Because when I got to the checkout counter, I realized I had bought two power lunches and together they cost almost $27.

So I started to slow my roll.

Sushi roll, that is.

But still, I like everything about our new modern way of living, which is that other people live for you and you just buy it and take it home.

Cooking is a great pleasure and all that, but it's nice to spread the pleasure around, don't you think?

But it's a slippery slope, friends.

Next thing you know, they'll prepare my dinner, chew it for me, and regurgiate it into my open beak.

I mean, mouth.

The only bad thing is when it comes to something like watermelon.

I'm unhappy about the state of watermelons these days. I don't know if it's genetic modification or world domination, but somebody is messing with the watermelons to make them seedless.

This isn't progress.

Let me tell you something.

I grew up eating watermelon and spitting the seeds everywhere.

It was fun.

I even had contests with my brother to see who could spit the seeds the farthest.

I won.

I love to spit, and seeds give me an excuse.

Bottom line, seed-spitting is good clean family time, and nobody should be taking the seeds out of watermelon.

On the contrary, somebody should be figuring out how to put more seeds in watermelon.

Think of all the fun we could have!

Who said you can't play with your food?

I can, if they let me.

So in review, I'm of two minds, which is a fancy way of saying I can't make up my one mind.

On the one hand, I love when everybody

prepares food for me, even if it cost too much.

On the other, I don't like when somebody prepares the food so much that they ruin our fun.

It's all food for thought!

CHALLENGED

FRANCESCA

"I want someone who challenges me" is one of those things people say about dating that I never fully believe.

I want someone who doesn't challenge me.

Now, don't misunderstand me. Of course I want to be with my intellectual equal, and I want my partner to feel free to speak his mind and disagree with me. But in general, I prefer a less contentious model for relationships. I've met too many guys who confuse snark for charm and combativeness for banter. I'm not all that big on teasing. I'd rather be my boyfriend's best friend, biggest supporter, and soft place to fall, and to have that in return.

But maybe I just had a poor introduction to the notion.

I dated a guy in college who often told me, "I can't date someone who doesn't challenge me."

I didn't think of myself as a particularly argumentative type of person, I'm generally pretty conflict-avoidant, but I understood he meant it as a compliment. He thought I was smart and confident, and I liked that he liked that about me. He was the first person I dated at Harvard, so I thought it was just a thing college guys said.

I didn't realize it was a trap.

The first time I fell for it, we were watching TV and an Aflac commercial came on.

"That voice is so funny. I wonder who they get to do that voice?" asked my boyfriend.

"It's Gilbert Gottfried," I said.

He shook his head. "Nah."

"Yeah, it is. You know, the guy who was the parrot in *Aladdin*? He's the Aflac duck."

"There is no way they'd pay all that money to get a celebrity to do it when any voice actor could for less."

In retrospect, this was prescient. But at the time, he was dead wrong.

"I don't know how expensive Gilbert Gottfried is, but it makes sense to me that they'd pay for him. It's a national ad campaign, they want a recognizable voice."

"There's no way."

"Well, I know he's the voice, so." I shrugged.

"I'm looking it up right now." He tapped away at his laptop for a few minutes, and then looked up at me in awe. "Oh my God, you're right."

I laughed lightly. "I told you, I knew who it was."

He smiled and kissed me. "And you know everything, right?"

I frowned. That wasn't what I'd meant. And I felt guilty — was that how I had come off?

Another night, we were lying in my bed watching one of the late-night shows (this was pre-Netflix-and-chill), and Jack Hanna was the guest.

My boyfriend pointed at the screen. "What animal is that, a lemur?"

"That's a sloth."

"I'm pretty sure that's a lemur."

"Lemurs have big eyes and stripes on their tails, like a 'ring-tailed lemur.' That's a sloth. Look how slow it's moving, hence the name — sloth, slow, lazy."

He screwed up his face. "Hold up. You're telling me they named the *sin* after an animal?"

"No, they named the animal after the sin."

We squinted at each other for a moment.

Then he laughed. "You're so crazy. I don't know what a sloth looks like, but I know it's not that."

"If you've never seen one, how are you so sure I'm wrong?"

"Because a sloth is a slimy, small thing, like a bug!"

"You mean a slug?"

"Oh, wait." He got on Google again, searched the word "sloth," and immediately hit results that looked exactly like the animal onscreen. He glanced up at me. "Look at that smile, you love this!"

"Love what?"

"You love to prove me wrong!"

"No, I don't! You just argue with me over things that I know to be true."

"It's okay, don't worry. Lucky for you, I like a challenge."

I didn't, I found these arguments tedious and exhausting. But I still felt like it was my fault somehow, and I wanted to prove I wasn't an obnoxious know-it-all. So I stuck it out with him and vowed to be more careful.

The final straw came after my birthday. I had three-day-old balloons in my room that had begun to wilt. One floated near my head and a few of my hairs rose up to meet it. He teased me about it.

"Oh, it must be the static electricity," I said. I saw the now-familiar skepticism flicker across his face. "Like how you can rub a balloon on your head and it will stick to the wall."

"What are you talking about?"

"I'm sure you've seen it before. It's like a six-year-old's idea of a party trick."

"Oh, so I'm dumb as a six-year-old?"

"No, I only meant —"

"If you're so smart, prove it." He pulled one of the balloons down from the ceiling and handed it to me.

I snatched the balloon from his hand, rubbed it on my head, and shoved it to the wall.

It stuck like glue.

I've genuinely never seen this trick work better than it did that day. Even the wall was tired of this guy's shtick.

"Whoa-hoh-ho. Since when do *you* know about science?"

I sighed. "I go to this school, too, remember?"

"I know, but c'mon." He gave a roll of his eyes. "You're an *English major.*"

Lord, grant me the confidence of a man who will condescend to the woman who just made a fool out of him.

Because he didn't really expect me, an *English major* and a woman, to be as smart as he was, certainly not smarter (if Gilbert

Gottfried trivia can possibly qualify as smarts). I was only supposed to be intelligent enough to reflect well on him. He liked a challenge as long as he ultimately won.

At least I think that's how he felt. I'll never know for sure if he actually enjoyed the tug-of-war.

I broke up with him too soon to find out.

Dumbing myself down was too much of a challenge.

HEAT WAVERING

LISA

I found out something bad about myself and I'm here to confess.

I'm an air-conditioner tyrant.

Let me explain.

We begin when Francesca comes home from New York so we could record the audiobook of *I Need a Lifeguard Everywhere but the Pool,* so you can listen to it when you drive around, and you have not known bliss until you have our two Philadelphia accents in your ear on a long car ride.

You're welcome.

Anyway, when Francesca comes home, in the middle of a weeklong heat wave, the first thing she notices is that I don't have the air-conditioning on.

That was a surprise ending, wasn't it?

You thought I was going to say that I *do* have the air conditioner on.

But in fact, one of the quirky things about me is that I don't like air-conditioning.

Quirky means adorable.

I don't know why I started hating on air-conditioning, but I always have. Even though I have central air-conditioning, I never use it.

Please allow me to defend myself.

I don't like feeling like I live inside a refrigerator. I like being the same temperature as my surroundings. And I love to throw open all the windows in the house and let in not only the breeze, but the chirping of the birds and the fresh green smell of mown grass.

I know, I'm so poetic.

Never mind that I'm sweating my ass off.

It's a poetic ass.

I don't know what to tell you, but I just like fresh air, and the most I do to get cool is put on a fan.

It's a $20 Lasko fan that you can buy at Home Depot, and I own approximately eight of them. I know it's not a classy look for the house. When I take a picture for my author page on Facebook, I make sure the fans don't show.

For my fans.

Plus I'm nostalgic about fans because they remind me of Mother Mary, and she and I used to have a famous fight, wherein she would claim that the fan should be in the window and turned blowing out, so the hot air was sucked out of the room.

Which sucked.

We sweated inside the house, cooling the backyard.

She also believed that you could put two fans in opposite windows and create cross-ventilation, but if you're relying on The Flying Scottolines for physics, you're in trouble.

So when I grew up, I decided that I would have the fans facing the way God intended, blowing air right at you. And then I got the brilliant idea that a fan didn't need to be in a window at all, but can be sitting right on the kitchen island next to you while you eat dinner.

Never mind that the fan will send tomato sauce spraying on to your T-shirt.

Think of it as a sea breeze, only Italian.

So as soon as Francesca comes home, she starts lobbying for me to turn on the air-conditioning, and I refuse. I tell her about the fans and Mother Mary and how great it is to feel the wind in your face, even if you bought the wind at Home Depot.

Francesca lets me have my way until the temperature turns 92° outside, a fact she proves by pointing to the air-conditioner thermostat. "Mom, do you see this? This is very hot. We need to turn on the air conditioner."

"No we don't. I feel fine. Sit in front of the fan."

"I am and I'm still hot."

"But I hate air-conditioning."

"I love air-conditioning. Mom, can't you compromise, just a little?"

"No," I tell her, meaning it. I hate compromising, too. I've spent my whole life compromising and now I avoid it at every opportunity.

And it feels great.

Even if I'm sweaty.

And you are, too.

You might think I'm a bad person, but I'm just a woman who has put everyone else first for a long time, and now it's my turn.

If you're a woman reading this, perhaps you identify. And if you don't, you've lived your life better than I have.

But then Francesca said to me, "Mom, look at the dogs, they're panting."

So I looked over on the kitchen floor, and Francesca was right. All six dogs had their tongues out, even though they had their own fan. And then I realized I could give my dogs heatstroke inside my own house.

So I compromised and turned on the air-conditioning.

And I learned something bad about myself.

That I compromised for my dogs, but not for my daughter.

A fact which I pointed out to Francesca, who just laughed.

But I learned a lesson.

Sometimes compromising is okay.

But don't make a habit of it.

And don't compromise a lot.

Only by degrees.

WHAT ARE THE ODDS?

LISA

Women worry.

Men worry too, but let's be honest, not as much.

They can't help it, they lack estrogen.

I've never known a man who worried as much as I do.

We begin with my late father, Frank, whom I adored, mainly because he never worried about anything.

He always said, "Everything is going to turn out all right in the end."

And you know, he was right.

So if something came up that would make me worry, I would worry worry worry until the end, and then everything turned out all right.

If you were my dad and something came up, he never worried and everything turned out all right.

See what I mean?

In between the bad thing and the end,

there was worry, if you were me.

And if you were my dad, you were smiling.

So whenever I start worrying about things, I tell myself to be like my dad and remember that everything is going to be all right. This had been working for me so far, until we came to my latest worry.

Lightning.

Laugh all you want, but lately I'm worrying about lightning striking my house.

And as soon as I started to worry about that, I realized that lightning is probably the perfect example of something that is crazy to worry about.

Every bad thing in the world is measured in terms of likelihood against a lightning strike. So is every good thing. As in, you have a better chance of getting struck by lightning than winning the lottery.

Yet I play the lottery every week.

So why aren't I worried about lightning strikes?

Obviously, I should be.

I'm underachieving in the worry category.

And I say this because, sadly, a friend of mine in another part of the country had a lightning strike on his house. I felt so terrible for him and sent him a note, but I told myself that probably wouldn't happen to me, because I don't live where he lives.

But one week after that, lightning struck a fence post in my backyard. It must've happened during the night, and I didn't see it until I went out back. The post had exploded into wooden pieces that were scattered everywhere, with black burn marks on them.

Worried, yet?

And then I remembered that three years ago, lightning had struck a tree in my front yard, and it fell over onto the garage roof. Amazingly, there was no damage and I was able to save half the tree, but there it stood outside my kitchen window, saying, You think lightning doesn't strike twice?

It does at my house.

I'm so tempted to make a Thing One and Thing Two joke, but at this point, you can fill that in for yourself. I know you can. Not everybody can compare their marriages to natural disasters, so I'm lucky in that regard.

Anyway, I called up a lightning-rod guy, and he came over and answered all my questions, like, do lightning rods attract lightning (no), what do they look like (spikes or balls on a stick), and what color do the balls come in (I'll get back to you).

Yes, I actually asked him, "What color are your balls?"

Also I had thought that I didn't need a lightning rod on the house because it was "grounded," a term I heard someone use once and still don't know the meaning of. But he explained that even though the house is grounded, it can still get struck by lightning and burn to the ground.

Truly, grounded.

So actually I wasn't worrying enough.

He gave me an estimate to install lightning rods, but it wasn't cheap and I wasn't sure what to do.

I mean, did I need them? Or was I worrying uselessly, as usual?

So I turned to the Internet for answers.

I know, I'm lazy.

So what follows is generally unreliable, and remember, this is a humor book.

It said online that the odds of being struck and killed by lighting is 1 in 74,000.

But it didn't say anything about the odds of a house getting struck by lightning, so I tried to evaluate other odds.

For example, the odds of getting attacked by a shark are one in 11.5 million.

Good to know.

Still staying out of the water.

I can never forget *Jaws*.

And the odds of winning the Powerball are one in 175,223,520.

Yet I play every week.

And intend to win.

Finally, I learned that the odds of getting killed in a plane crash are one in 9,700.

Wait, what?

Okay, that's way too high.

No wonder I'm afraid to fly.

When I win the Powerball, I'm buying a plane and a really big mattress to fly right underneath it in case, well, you know.

So what did I learn from my research?

Nothing.

Regardless of reality, I worry, and I worry about all the wrong things.

So I decided to get the lightning rods.

Even if it will be all right in the end.

Thanks, Dad.

LOVE BITES
FRANCESCA

Mosquitoes love me.

I've always believed I get an inordinate number of mosquito bites, but I never said it out loud. Everyone feels this way. Brandish a bottle of OFF! at any summer barbecue, and five people will proclaim that mosquitoes love them with equal parts self-pity and pride. It's almost a humble-brag, as if mosquitoes are real aesthetes, the bloodsucking playboys of the insect world.

The subtext is: "There's just something about my exposed skin that attracts all species, whatta hassle!"

Then I recently came across an article explaining mosquitoes actually do have a "type": they're most attracted to humans with the blood type O.

My blood type.

I wasn't imagining it, it wasn't some messed-up version of vanity, it was science!

Mosquitoes don't consciously know

they're looking for O blood or even why they prefer it, they've simply evolved to blindly seek out what's good for them.

It got me thinking, how much of finding what we need is pure animal attraction? And why are we so quick to dismiss our instincts as unsophisticated or undiscerning?

There's not enough animal attraction in dating these days. Now we have apps using data analytics and algorithms to help us find partners. Technology is helping us meet, but is it helping us mate?

How many of us have swiped right on someone with all the right stats and pictures, only to find you two have zero chemistry in person?

Smartphones are no match for pheromones.

In the old days, like pre-Tinder 2012, we had to meet out in the wild, at local watering holes, places where we could get within sniffing distance of one another and let the limbic brain do its work.

This is essentially how I've met every man I ended up in a serious relationship with. It was never a calculated, well-thought-out assessment of the man in front of me, it was just an immediate, inexplicable attraction, like getting hit by a two-by-four, if the two-by-four were made of warm feelings instead of wood.

My attraction couldn't have been solely based on looks because while they were all Studly Do-Rights to me, they looked completely different from one another.

I thought the fact that my exes have nothing superficial in common proved that I was sensitive and deep. But maybe I'm no more evolved than the humble mosquito, subliminally picking up on advantageous genetic matches.

Even if we didn't procreate, hey, it was fun while it lasted.

Likewise, I think I'm more attractive in person than online. I don't photograph that well, I hunch to cuddle up to friends, and I don't know what to do with my nose. But when I go out, I tend to meet men easily. I'd developed my own theories as to why:

I'm smiley and approachable. Some people have "resting bitch face," I must have "resting slut face."

My looks fall in that sweet spot between sort-of-pretty but not scary-pretty. Maybe it's the curly hair. Sleek, bombshell blowouts make a woman too intimidating. I know, because when I get a great blowout, I get delusions of grandeur. I start thinking things like, "Should I date a professional athlete?" and "How does one meet Jake Gyllenhaal?"

My crazy, natural curls communicate something more accessible to men, like, "I might have lost my keys."

Or could it be my sparkling personality?

Nah. It is just as likely my blood type, or some other genetic quality completely out of my control.

Bruised ego aside, wouldn't that be kind of freeing? The notion that there's nothing we need to do or change about ourselves to attract our ideal mate — not losing five pounds, or choosing the right outfit, or coming up with the perfect opening line. Instead, something buried deep in our DNA will guide us to the person we need.

It's almost romantic.

So I say we need to take a lesson from the mosquito, a bug of taste, and return to letting animal attraction lead the way.

In the meantime, can somebody please pass the calamine?

A Woman with a Plan

LISA

I'm not a planner.

But I got a letter from my local funeral home, asking that I plan a funeral.

For myself.

I tried not to be insulted.

I mean, do I look that bad?

I might, since I just finished a draft of my next novel, and the truth is that daily showers, nutrition, and grooming go by the wayside when I'm on deadline.

Of course, deadline takes on a whole new meaning when your funeral home is sending you love letters.

The letter offered to save me 44 percent on funeral or cremation costs.

This would be the ultimate final sale.

But to take advantage, I have to decide right now if I want to be buried or reduced to ash.

Are we having fun yet?

The letter said that the sale price was

"guaranteed, no-increase pricing."

To which I thought, You're darn tootin'.

Try and collect after I'm dead.

Oh, wait. Maybe you can.

The only things guaranteed are death and taxes, and there are taxes after death, so why not a price hike?

I just wish they'd hike me out of the ground.

Maybe that should be my epitaph:

GET ME OUT OF HERE.

How about, I GOT THIS 44% OFF. ASK ME HOW.

Or, I'D RATHER DIE THAN PAY FULL PRICE.

The letter said I should take the deal because it would "protect positive memories" for my family.

That's my kind of sales pitch.

In other words, buy this, so your family won't be pissed that you left them holding the bag.

You old bag.

The letter called it a Prearranged Funeral Program, which, I have to admit, appealed to my vanity.

It's not a funeral, it's a show!

The Bye-bye, Lisa Show!

Unfortunately there's only one episode.

The premiere and the finale are the same thing.

Bring a lot of popcorn.

It's not a surprise ending.

You might even cry.

At least, you'd better.

You guys, when I die, I want you all there, sobbing your eyes out. Saying how wonderful I was. And also what a smart shopper.

"Her books are great, plus she got a deal on the casket!"

But I'm not sure I want a half-price deal on a casket.

Maybe you don't get a lid.

You get a tray.

Or maybe you *only* get a lid and they flip you over like a cake you just took out of the oven.

If you follow.

None of these jokes apply to cremation, which is inherently unfunny.

I don't even like hot water.

Or a sunburn.

Ouchie.

Cremation goes against our natural instincts, doesn't it?

We tell every child, "Don't put your hand in fire."

But someday you'll get a letter that says, "See that fire? Jump in!"

Really, the letter is offering a fire-sale price on an actual fire.

How meta.

This is the best part of the letter: "In short, don't put it off. As more time passes, the more your loved ones could end up paying for this kind of security."

HAHAHAHA.

Tick-tock, Scottoline.

Don't delay because you could die any minute.

And it's gonna cost somebody 44 percent more.

You selfish bitch.

I mean, that puts the fun in funeral.

But in the end, I'm going to take advantage of the offer.

I can't pass up a sale.

And I like to clean up after myself, so to speak.

So maybe I'm a planner, after all.

I've become one, after a lifetime.

Literally.

Plus I have loyalty to the funeral home, since they buried my father and mother. And when they came to pick up my mother the morning she passed, there were tears in their eyes, and they actually said, "Is this the famous Mother Mary?"

Aw.

So you know they have my business, from now on.

Because they read me.

People who read my books are my second-favorite people on the planet.

My most favorite are people who *buy* my books.

Why?

Who do you think is paying to put me in an ashtray, at a date yet to be determined?

I sincerely hope it's you.

You'll be happy to know I got you a deal.

Thank you for your support.

Now, and later.

No More Sex and No More City

LISA

I know, I should let it go.

But I can't.

And I won't.

By now you have heard the bad news.

There will not be a *Sex and the City 3*.

Or to those of us in the know, SATC3.

For those of you youngsters, I'm talking about American history.

In other words, the television series *Sex and the City,* which followed the adventures of four women in New York City, which ran from 1998 to 2004 on television.

Its star was Carrie Bradshaw, played by the wonderful Sarah Jessica Parker, who played a columnist, but the series was a true girl ensemble, with Miranda, Charlotte, and Samantha.

Miranda was the cynical one.

Charlotte was the preppy one.

Samantha was the sexy one.

I loved the series, and so did Francesca,

and we owned something called DVDs, which you can still find somewhere in your house, but will not be able to play anymore.

What we loved about the show was how wonderful the individual characters were and how close they were, while also experiencing the ebb and flow in female friendship, as well as career ups and downs and romantic entanglements.

In other words, women in real life.

After the series was over, they made a movie, *Sex and the City,* which Francesca and I loved.

And they made another movie *Sex and the City 2,* which Francesca and I also loved.

So you're getting the idea.

We're fans.

We're loyal.

The only movie I've been as true a fan of was *The Godfather* movies, and of course I loved I, II, and III.

Nobody liked *Godfather 3* except me.

I even read an interview with an actual godfather who said that movie sucked.

But I disagree.

Because my fanhood goes deep.

I feel the same way about *Sex and the City,* but just this week, it was announced that there would be no third movie.

Reportedly, Kim Catrall, the actress who

played Samantha, did not want to do a third one because she wasn't sure they were "relevant anymore."

I don't know if that is true.

They were still relevant to me, and probably to Francesca, but I'll speak for myself now.

They were so relevant it wasn't even funny.

Because you might be hard-pressed to name any all-female franchise in television or movies, at all.

Although there are certainly plenty of buddy films, superhero movies, and comic-book heroes.

And I'm from Philly, a city that plays *Rocky 1* through 55 on a continuous loop in almost every ballpark, bar, and restaurant.

One thing that was so great about *Sex and the City* was simply about representation.

How often do women see themselves as main characters on TV and film?

How often are female friendships given the status in art that we give it in real life?

And while we're on the subject, how about Cosmos?

There ain't nothing wrong with a Cosmo.

There is no way you have a bad time when you're holding a Cosmo.

It's simply the most potent pink lemonade possible.

Don't try to say that sentence after a few Cosmos.

As in two.

The shape of the Cosmo glass alone is a hoot.

To a writer like me, the telling detail is everything.

And I think that the Cosmo was the telling detail of the series.

Because it showed women having fun together, giving each other the gift of their own time, and just talk, talk, talking over food and drink.

Is that the stuff of most women's friendships?

And hasn't it sustained most of us through divorces, diagnoses, the birth of children, and the subsequent strep throats, soccer schedules, and several hundred Things To Do lists?

I will tell you that the greatest blessing of my life, in addition to my wonderful daughter, is an amazing group of girlfriends. And I bet, if you pause to think about it, that you feel the same way.

We women are so lucky to have each other.

We serve as a female force field, like a cloak of immunity against life's trials.

And not just on girls' night out, if you're lucky to have one of those.

But in all the in-between times, the quick phone calls and quicker texts, the touching-base and catching-up, all the ways in which women, as practical as we are, can always manage to wedge even more into an already busy day.

We're marvels, truly.

We live days that would flatten lesser mortals.

And nobody knows it but each other.

I celebrate us.

I celebrate all of you, and your girlfriends.

So maybe we don't have *Sex and the City* anymore.

But we still have each other.

And will always have Cosmos.

Francesca Serritella, Attorney at Paw

My mom recently shared how I successfully advocated for the dogs to get air-conditioning in the house, but you may not know that this was merely the latest in a string of victories for Francesca Serritella, Attorney at Paw.

I've always acted as the lawyer for our pets. Maybe because I was an only child, I viewed the pets as animal siblings, voiceless against unchecked parental authority. Also, when I would throw a tantrum as a little girl, my mom would say: "Argue your case, convince me." It was a great way to force me to calm down, think through my position, and, on occasion, admit defeat.

I learned my lesson well, and unfortunately for my mother, she got an amateur trial lawyer for a daughter. My chosen field is animal advocacy.

I practice family law. When my mom added two puppies to our family four years ago, I could see the living situation had become untenable for our cat, Mimi.

Our other cat, Vivi, chose not to retain my services. She enjoys taunting the dogs and settled out of court.

But Mimi was another story. I recognized that her lounging rights were being infringed upon, her sun-spots had been unlawfully seized, and the increased barking constituted a noise violation the homeowner failed to rectify.

Working together with CPS, Cat Protection Services — also headed by me — I successfully negotiated for a better home placement for Mimi.

In my apartment.

As terms of the separation, Mimi won possession of the cat carrier, and the defendant had to fund the first year of medical services, such as vaccines and feline dental work, so that Mimi could live in the manner to which she was accustomed.

The divorce was finalized a few years ago. She's Mimi Serritella now.

Sadly, her alimony has ceased.

I also specialize in disability law for our handicapped corgi, Ruby. To be fair, my mom has always been amenable, as she adores the dog. But Ruby has been my client for many years.

Long before Ruby became paralyzed, I insisted my mom buy Ruby stairs so she could get up on my mom's bed. We can't discriminate against corgis for having legs like meaty drumsticks. Animals shaped like pork roasts aren't well equipped for jumping. The bed must be accessible to all dogs in the house.

Wooden stairs to the bed were purchased, and an important precedent was set. Ruby's bed privileges became the law of the land. And I have fought tirelessly to ensure those bed rights remain intact.

Now, with her paralysis, Ruby is incontinent. I came home for a visit and saw that my mom was having her sleep downstairs at night.

I objected. "She's never slept downstairs. All the dogs get to go upstairs with you and be in the bed. They're pack animals, you can't single her out. She feels like she's being punished."

My mom had a decent rebuttal. "Ruby poops during the night, in my bed, and the fan blows the smell right in my face."

"Fan — you're not using the A/C?"

So Ruby's back in the bed. She wears a diaper and sleeps on a wee-wee pad.

I also worked on upgrading her vehicle. Since her rear-leg function began to deteriorate, she's been through several different wheel carts to help her get around. Sadly, these days, her front legs aren't up to the task of pulling herself in a cart. So she hangs out on a dog bed that we move from room to room with us.

She's actually quite happy, because corgis can supervise the universe from anywhere.

Except when it comes to family dog-walks. Typically, when I visit and provide another set of hands for wrangling, we take all the pups out for a big walk around the country roads. But now that Ruby can no longer manage her cart, she can't come along.

Once again, I thought the state could do more. "We have to get her a dog-stroller!" I cried. I'd seen people in the city use them for their old dogs. I quickly pulled up several options online, some of which cost over $150.

"She doesn't need a stroller," my mom said. "I don't take them for walks that often."

"She can use it in the house too, then you won't have to bend over and drag her bed around."

"I'm fine dragging her. And we have to be honest, I'm not sure how much longer this will be an issue."

I used an effective, if unorthodox, argument tactic: I burst into tears.

"So we'll use it for her last walk. She deserves that," I said through my sobs.

Soon, my mom was crying too, vowing that Ruby has many more walks ahead of her, and expediting the shipping of her brand-new stroller.

Life is unfair. Dogs don't live forever. Cats get dog siblings they never wanted. Even alpha dogs' bodies let them down. Pets need an advocate to tip the scales toward justice.

I love these animals. I'll always have their furry backs.

My secret to legal victory?

My mom loves them just as much.

The Case of the Missing Eyebrows

LISA

Something is missing from my life.

My eyebrows.

You thought I was going to say sex.

But I'm talking about something I actually miss.

Although to be fair, I didn't even notice my eyebrows were missing.

Which gives you an idea of how often I look in a mirror.

That's a tip, for those of you who are aging.

Don't look.

You'll think you're young.

Your brain won't know you're a hag.

Sorry, I hope I didn't offend any hags.

Because I am one, and I think it might be the greatest word ever.

I think we should start owning our hagdom.

Anyway, to get back to my eyebrows, I didn't really notice they were missing until I was getting a new author photo, which I make sure happens every decade.

I use an author photo until it breaks Photoshop.

A makeup artist came to my house for the photo shoot, took one look at me, and said, "Your eyebrows need filling in."

Oh, the indignities of old age.

Your brows need filling in, but your waist doesn't.

So she got some pencils and drew eyebrows on me, like new roofs for my eyes.

That's the problem with home improvement.

It doesn't stop at your home.

The makeup artist liked my new eyebrows, but I didn't, since I had gotten used to looking like the clown in *It.*

I told myself, think of the bright side!

You're in the movies!

Also, it took forever to build my new roof-eyebrows because there's a lot of variations in eyebrows.

Who knew?

Who cared?

First the makeup artist made them too thick.

I looked like Angry Bird.

Then she thinned them out.

I looked like Boris Badenov.

We settled on thinner still, so at least I got to be Natasha.

Whose last name is Fatale, by the way.

So maybe she's Italian?

And eyebrow color was an issue too.

The makeup artist had seven different eyebrow pencils, all of which looked brown to me.

I suggested we go with mousey brown, since that was the color my eyebrows used to be and probably why I don't miss them.

She preferred blond, since it went with my highlights.

HAHAHAHAHAHAHA.

So if the carpet doesn't match the drapes, change the carpet.

It got me thinking about where my eyebrows went, and I found myself on The Case of the Missing Eyebrows.

Like Nancy Drew, in menopause.

Actually, I'm so much of a hag that I don't even remember menopause.

I'm past menopause, if such a thing is even possible.

Like if you're past menopause, you might be dead.

I actually miss menopause.

Those hot flashes kept me warm in winter.

I saved on my oil bill.

Also I didn't have to shower because I was

always wet.

Again, look on the bright side!

Menopause saves money!

In fact, I remember menopause more fondly than my eyebrows.

Maybe menopause and my eyebrows are in the same place, yukking it up over the fact that they ditched me.

Like Boris and Natasha, they're no-goodniks.

I'm realizing now that it's odd to think about being past menopause, only because you never hear anything about it.

Past menopause must be Hag Central.

Of course you hear a lot about perimenopause, which is what happens before menopause, when you're still young enough to matter.

HAHAHAHAHAHAHA.

I have younger friends who talk about being in perimenopause, with horror.

Brace yourself, sister.

You'll be in and out of peri in no time.

Perimenopause is like starter menopause.

It's warming you up for warming up.

Also, everything you read about perimenopause says that it lasts ten years, but I don't believe that for a minute.

I think perimenopause exists because

nobody wants to admit they're in meno-pause.

Because that sounds too haggy.

Like forty is the new fifty, menopause-wise.

Of course, that's not a medical opinion.

Please remember this is a humor column.

I'm no gynecologist.

I may not even have a vagina anymore.

God knows where that girl is these days.

But I'm here to tell you that even though nobody talks about it, being postmeno-pausal is great.

You don't sweat, flash, or feel hot any-more.

You're finally cool.

In fact, being a hag is very cool.

You'll see.

BHUTAN BOUND

LISA

There's a new tourist destination, but I'm not going there.

Bhutan.

Where is that?

It's a country in Asia, between Tibet and India.

Why won't I go there?

Because Bhutan is the land of the phallus.

What?

You read that right.

I was reading the newspaper, and I happened to come across an article that talked about how Bhutan is a country that is basically decorated in penis.

In other words, there are sunflowers in Tuscany and lavender in Provence, but in Bhutan, it's all about penis.

I know, ladies, it occasionally feels that way at home too, but I'll set my feminism aside for the moment.

Apparently, people in Bhutan have pictures of penises everywhere. They paint them on their houses and they put them above their doorways.

I was going to say mount them.

They even carve penises out of wood and sell them.

That would be the original woody.

They even wear them on necklaces, like a charm.

Yes, a penis pendant.

Charming.

I mean, what woman wouldn't want one?

He got it at Jared.

No, actually, it *is* Jared.

They even make really big penises and put them in the fields to use as scarecrows.

I'm not talking six inches, I'm talking six feet.

That, I get.

If I saw a six-foot-tall penis in a field, I'd fly away, too.

But I don't think they're giving the crows any credit.

Those birds aren't scared, they're grossed out.

They're like, let's go to Tuscany.

Sunflowers!

And I can imagine the conversations between the penis-scarecrows, fighting about which is bigger.

Anyway, back to my ace reporting about Bhutan.

According to the article, a Bhutanese writer explained that the penises "remind onlookers that if this force is harnessed properly, it will fuel productivity and creativity rather than wanton lust."

I'm not sure I'm buying that.

I think when people think about a penis, they're more likely to think in the Wanton Lust category rather than the Productivity and Creativity category.

Plus I don't know about you, but I don't want to harness a penis.

I honestly don't think I could.

I can't even get a collar on the dogs without them barking and running around like nuts.

The Bhutanese believe that the penis brings good luck.

Okay, let's stop right there.

You know who spreads this belief?

People with penises.

I can tell you right now, penises do not always bring good luck.

My luck is a lot better without the penis.

In my experience, the penis always wants its own way.

To be fair, what else would you expect from a penis?

I mean, they're bossy.

They were born that way.

Freud famously said that women have penis envy, but he was completely wrong.

Because he was a man, and therefore unqualified to tell anybody what women want, particularly women.

I'll tell you what women want.

Somebody to take out the recycling.

We do not want the penis.

Especially yours.

Have you looked at it lately?

You'd have to be blind to want to look at a penis.

By the way, it's become clear to me by now that men do not understand this.

They're under the completely mistaken impression that their penis is something women want to see. This is the only possible explanation for why they keep sending photos of them to women.

I think that's the basic difference between women and men.

A pretty woman will look in a mirror and think she's not worthy of being looked at.

A man will look at the ugliest part of his body and be absolutely certain that everybody wants to see it.

I don't fault men for this.

On the contrary, I admire them.

I wish women had that self-confidence.

Then we could establish a country where we paint vaginas on the houses.

And carve vaginas out of wood.

And wear vaginas around our necks.

With matching earrings, one ovary for each ear.

And in this magical country, the vaginas could actually make the same pay as the penises.

Now that's the country I would visit.

But I still wouldn't go in the fields.

Out of Order

FRANCESCA

In my home, a few things are temporarily out of order.

Permanently.

I intend to fix them someday. It's just not urgent.

But *not urgent* becomes *never* faster than you think.

Maybe if I confess to you in writing, it will shame me into doing something.

The first issue was apparent as soon as I moved in: the stair railing. The metal banister on the second floor has no bottom rail, leaving a foot-high space exposed to the stairwell. This did not pass my dog-safety standards. I had terrifying visions of Pip chasing a toy, slipping under it, and tumbling down to the floor below.

I don't delay when there's danger to my dog-child.

So the first day, I taped cardboard on the lowest rung of the railing down to the floor, forming a protective base wall. It wasn't pretty, but it would keep Pip safe until I found a better solution.

That was five years ago.

The irony is, I took great care to decorate the rest of my apartment like a classy adult — I repainted, I put up art — and yet my cardboard safety wall remains, now with stains and dog hair clinging to the curling packing tape.

I don't even see it anymore. I vacuum against it as if it's an elegant baseboard.

Is denial a design aesthetic?

And there's the practical reason — money. It would be a big, expensive job to replace the banister.

Not that I've really looked into it.

I did look into fixing my tub drain. It's got the winning combination of never sealing tightly for baths, yet draining too slowly for showers. I hired a plumber, but he said it was a flaw in the installation, and the only way to fix it would be to rip out the tub and break into the marble tile to reach the pipes.

Or, I could buy two plastic drain covers at the hardware store, one flat and one a basket, for about ten bucks.

Tough call!

If it's not money preventing me from fixing the broken thing, it's burnout. I took forever choosing the perfect pendant light to go over my dining table. When I finally found a stylish and affordable one, I felt so proud of myself. Mission accomplished!

I forgot I needed an electrician to install it.

Productivity is like a cell-phone battery, it runs out when you need it most.

Since I'd lived without a dining-table light during my lengthy search, I had gotten used to the dim lighting.

It makes eating alone romantic.

And let's be real, my cooking isn't Instagram-worthy.

So my pendant light became a decorative object, sitting at the center of my table for the next two years.

But I know, I'm making excuses. My inclination to just live with problems instead of always taking action is one of my worst qualities. All I can say is, I'm working on it.

Eventually.

Am I the only one like this?

Certainly not in my family. My dad's house had a bathroom that was missing its sink for years, but it was close enough to the kitchen that we just washed our hands there.

Don't tell the Department of Health.

My aunt and uncle have a toilet with a

chain-pull flush so temperamental, they have flushing instructions framed and hung beside it.

You know you're committed to your broken thing when you post signage.

At my mom's house, it's the downstairs toilet. Often, when flushed, the plug in the tank doesn't seal and it runs continuously, spelling doom for the septic tank.

On my last visit, I was reading on the couch when my mom came in wearing her best "I'm not mad, I'm disappointed" face. She asked me if I had used the bathroom, and I told her I had.

"Well." She crossed her arms. "Were you rough with it?"

I shrugged. "No."

She sighed and gave me a skeptical look.

"Mom, I didn't *do* anything to it, it doesn't work sometimes — it's broken."

She looked almost hurt. "No, it's not broken. But you know how it is. You have to be gentle."

It sounded like she was defending a person instead of a toilet.

And maybe that's the reason we don't fix the permanently out-of-order things in our homes. We live with them and their quirks for so long, they feel like family. So we accept them, flaws and all.

Whether our problem is that we're cheap, or a little lazy, or our tank plug doesn't seal properly, we're trying our best.

Be gentle.

Nobody's perfect.

MONEY FOR NOTHING

LISA

My mail is pranking me.

Again.

I got my mail, and on top was a flat envelope with a clear window and perforations on the side, which can only mean one thing.

A check.

Before I begin, let me first say that I get a lot of checks in the mail, but before you get jealous, they're never for a lot of money.

Because I apply for every stupid rebate in the universe.

I've gotten checks for a dollar on rebates for batteries, lightbulbs, and flea and tick remedies.

Those are for the dogs.

I keep my fleas and ticks.

I also get little checks for class-action lawsuits.

Evidently, I've been victimized by a lot of big companies, because I'm always getting notices in the mail telling me that I'm part of a class-action lawsuit that I didn't even know about.

Maybe this means I'm classy.

So class-action lawyers are running around suing people, as God intended, and when they send me notices that I'm a member of the class, I fill out and send in the form.

I don't want you to get the idea I'm cheap, because I'm not.

I'm actually just stupid with money.

So there you have it.

I'm not cheap, I'm dumb.

For example, I don't use coupons at stores anymore because I kept forgetting them, and I don't keep track of my frequent-flyer miles, which I accumulate like crazy on book tour, because the last thing I want to do is fly anywhere else.

In other words, I don't do the big things to save a lot of money.

I do the little things that save tiny amounts of money.

Have you ever gotten one of those class-action checks?

Here's what you get a check for:

$.37

Sometimes it's as much as a dollar.

That would be like winning the class-action lottery.

I don't even know why I send in the form, except for the fact that way back in my lawyering days, I actually worked on a case in which somebody was a class-action member, neglected to send in the form, and therefore missed out on $100,000.

That's a true story.

I think of that every time I get my mail.

I think, maybe there will be a check for $100,000 inside, since, unbeknownst to me, I was completely victimized and in dire need of costly justice.

So because I do get checks in the mail that I don't recognize, I open up every piece of mail that looks like a check, whether I recognize it or not.

You know where this is going.

I get a lot of mail that looks exactly like a check, but then when I open it, I get excited because it looks exactly like a check.

But it's not.

I'm looking at one right now.

At the top it says in bold, **Funds Distribution Center**, which, at first glance, sounds official to me.

After all, it means there are funds and that I'm getting a distribution from something called a distribution center.

Then I gave it a second look.

And I realized a **Funds Distribution Center** is a bank.

But this check isn't from a bank.

The check has a pretty blue background, and it even says at the top, **Document Has A Colored Background**.

So maybe it really is for dumb people.

It also reads, **Security Features Listed On Back**.

So it has security features!

That sounds very checklike to me.

Doesn't it, to you?

As in, we need **security** at the **funds distribution center**!

On the upper right-hand side is a number, so it looks superofficial, or is at least, well, numbers.

Numbers = legit.

And on the lower right-hand side is a signature, written in a Flare pen.

Flares = legit.

Except that the name is illegible and there's no printed name underneath, which should've tipped me off.

It says **Authorized Signature**, but it doesn't say who it's the authorized signature of.

I'm guessing Jimmy Hoffa.

Please tell me you know who that is.

And the fake check is for $45,000.

Wow!

Somebody must really be victimizing me without my knowing.

Unfortunately, if you look closer at the signature, it says in small print underneath, **This Is Not A Check**.

Wait, what?

This is a check that is not a check.

Lawyers wrote that sentence.

So I turn over the back of my fake check, where it says **Consolidate Today And Save!**

And I learn that this is an ad for debt consolidation.

I'm trying to understand how this marketing works, because all it did was make me cranky.

I hate the company that sent this to me.

They tricked me so cruelly.

I thought I was going to get $45,000, and now I'm not.

You know what I'm going to do to spite them?

Rack up a lot of debt and sell it to somebody else.

That'll show them.

DIRTY

LISA

I'm behind the times, and I'm fine with that.

Let's start with sexting.

First, that's not a word.

No amount of saying it should make it a word.

I'm an author, and I get to say.

Not a word.

That said, I don't even know what it means. I assume that it means sending somebody a dirty text or picture.

By the way, dirty is a great word, and we should use it more

As in, sex is dirty.

See what I mean?

Behind the times.

Ask me if I care.

But what got me thinking about dirty pictures was the night I left my phone on a plane, and at the time, I wasn't using a passcode.

I didn't think I needed a passcode. My

days are spent in front of a computer, and I barely see another soul. The dogs are around, but none of them are interested in my phone.

But that night when I left my phone on the plane, my first thought was, somebody was going to see my pictures.

And they're not dirty.

In fact, that's what I was worried about.

I did recover the phone, which was evidently found abandoned in an airport café by whoever took it off the plane. When I got home, I looked at my phone, just to see what they had seen.

And I realized that my photos fall into two subjects.

Pets and body parts.

We'll start with the dogs because I want to keep you in suspense about the body parts.

My dogs dominate my photos, and they dominate me too. Practically every single picture is of the dogs, and I have four Cavalier King Charles spaniels and one aging corgi, who now wears a diaper.

How's she doing?

It depends.

Anyway, you could look at these pictures and marvel at why they were taken at all, because the dogs aren't doing anything worth taking a picture of.

And in my book, that's enough, for dogs.

Also cats.

I have plenty of cat pictures too, but they're all of her butt, since the only thing my cat does is walk away from me.

Most of the dog pictures are the dogs sleeping in various combinations on couches with quilts thrown on top, in a vain effort to preserve my furniture. If you follow me on social media, you know what I'm talking about, because all I do is post pictures of the dogs sleeping and try to think of funny captions to make them entertaining.

My dogs are slacking, social-media-wise.

If they didn't live with such a good writer, they would not be earning their keep.

But now we come to the other category of photos.

Body parts.

I don't have dirty pictures.

I have medical photos.

For example, my tongue has been bothering me lately, and by lately, I mean the past five years.

Yes, we're going there.

You're about to hear about my tongue problems.

Sometimes it swells and the doctors don't know why, but they say it's not cancer.

So there's the good news.

On the other hand, my tongue is swollen and that makes it hard to talk, which is my hobby.

Please recall I'm a woman.

Also it makes it hard to eat, so you feel me.

I'm getting frustrated that nobody can figure out what's wrong with my tongue, so every time it swells, I take a picture of myself with my tongue out to show the doctor.

It looks like bad porn.

I probably have thirty-five pictures of myself with my tongue out, which was my first thought when I realized that I lost my phone.

Somebody would think I was capable of only bad porn, when I'm pretty sure I could come up with mediocre porn.

If I really tried.

The other medical picture in my phone is equally disgusting.

If you're not a TMI fan, you should check out now.

On the other hand, if you read me with any regularity, you know that TMI is my favorite thing after Bradley Cooper.

I'm really hoping he reads this and wants to help with my tongue.

Because I think he could cure me.

Or at least I would stop caring.

In fact, I'm pretty sure that if Bradley Cooper called me, anything above the waist would be a waste of time.

See what I mean?

Mediocre porn.

And I wasn't even trying.

Anyway, the second type of medical photograph on my phone is of my eyelid. Since I am a hag nowadays, I have a weird little skin tag there that's getting longer and longer.

Have you thrown up yet?

I'll keep trying.

I asked the doctor about it the last time I was there, and she told me that it wasn't worth taking off.

Easy for her to say.

If this eye thing gets any bigger, I'm changing my name to Cyclops.

I'm on a campaign to convince my doctor that we should do something about the skin tag, so I take pictures of it to prove that it's growing. Unfortunately, it grows slowly, so there are easily three hundred pictures of my skin tag taken over the past five years.

That's how dirty my phone gets.

The final category of photographs in my phone is the pictures I take of myself accidentally, usually of my neck.

Ladies, need I explain?

You know what I'm talking about.

I wouldn't show my neck pictures even to a doctor.

I wonder what the guy who took my phone thought of them.

Come to think of it, maybe that's why he ditched it.

In some of the photos, you can't even recognize my neck as a human body part.

It's wrinkly, vaguely pinkish, and dotted with age spots.

I'm pretty sure that if you connected the dots, you'd have the Big and Little Dippers.

Sorry, that would be my breasts

BATTLESHIP NOODLE
FRANCESCA

I was talking to my mom on the phone on a beautiful, eighty-five-degree Saturday, and she asked me if I was going to the pool.

"Nah, I'd rather stay in and work. The pool is too stressful."

I'm a member of a fitness club that has a gorgeous rooftop pool. During summer in the city, there's nowhere you would rather be.

And that's the problem.

There are too many people.

If you give someone the choice between working out or lying on a deck chair in the sun, everyone will choose the latter. So it's a fight to find a spot. And there's nowhere the competition is fiercer than the area which borders the pool, where the chairs are not regular plastic chaises, but double-wide cushioned beds.

When people get one of those beds, they camp out for hours. I've gone without eating lunch to hold on to one.

My best friend and I were there the other day, and there wasn't a free chair in sight, not even in the shade next to the bathrooms. We laid our towels out directly on the concrete by the pool and waited for something to open up.

Side note, my friend is visibly pregnant, but no one was coughing up their chair.

I hated that she didn't have a more comfortable place to relax, so instead of relaxing myself, I remained vigilant.

Later, while we were chatting in the shallow end of the pool, I noticed a woman packing up her things on one of the bed-chairs right beside where we're standing. I pushed myself out of the pool so fast my bandeau top came down. A small price to pay to the roof-pool-gods. I yanked it back up without missing a beat.

"Are you leaving?" I asked.

She smiled and nodded, and I hovered, dripping wet, until she left and I jumped on it. These chairs are big enough for two to share, so I staked our claim while my friend went to get our towels.

I lay back, finally exhaling, when I heard a voice coming from the pool.

"That was rude."

I sat up to see a woman floating on a

noodle, glaring at me. "You're very rude," she repeated.

"Me?" I pointed at myself, bewildered. "How am I rude?"

"I was going to take that chair."

"Is your stuff here?" I looked around the area.

"No, my stuff is over there." She points to *a different chair,* admittedly one of the less desirable armchairs, but a cushioned one, and right by the pool. "But I was waiting to move to that one."

"Oh." I was confused. "Well, we've also been waiting for a chair."

"I had asked that woman for it when she was done with it." She paddled closer, still aboard her battleship noodle. "I believe you made an honest mistake, maybe you didn't know, but that wasn't very polite."

"I don't think we can really prenegotiate the chairs —"

"I could have jumped out of the pool and grabbed it, too."

I wanted to say, yes, you could have. Instead, I tried to say as nicely as possible, "I'm sorry. A chair opened up. We've been waiting for one. You actually already have a chair, my friend and I have none. I'm sorry for you that I got to this one first, but I don't see how I did anything wrong here."

"Listen, I'm not trying to start shit," she said loud enough for the whole pool to hear. "I'm not trying to *start shit* with you, I'm just letting you know that *you are rude.*"

I didn't know one could "start shit" from a purple noodle.

My friend returned with our towels. "Is everything okay?"

I tried to briefly catch her up on the situation while the woman floated in the water right before us, frowning behind big, black sunglasses. I spoke softly, "I mean, I think I've handled it at this point, but you know, there's . . . a little tension."

I shouldn't have even told her, my friend is way nicer than I am. "Well, if she really wants it, I guess something else will open up. I mean" — she lowered her voice — "is she just gonna stare at us?"

"I dunno," I muttered. "I'm fine, but I want you to be comfortable."

"I don't want the bad vibes."

I asked if she was sure, and she nodded. The injustice of it all irked me, but I sighed out my frustration. I gave the woman a little wave, as if she weren't already looking at us. "Miss? You know what, you can have the chair. We'll wait for the next one."

"No, it's fine," she said, folding her arms across her chest.

This. This is the ultimate girl-move. Having called me out in front of everyone, she would now rather passive-aggressively spite-float on her noodle.

"Look, I heard you, I had no idea you had discussed it with anyone, it was a misunderstanding. I'm a nice person, you're a nice person, it's too nice a day for hard feelings. So please, the chair is yours. We're going to swim around for a little longer."

She relinquished the HMS *Hate Noodle* and slowly waded over to the stairs out of the pool.

(As opposed to pushing herself up and out like a rude animal, I assume.)

"Thank you," she said.

I smiled. "No problem. And how 'bout this, when you're done with it, give us a holler? We'll take it after you."

"I'll let you know," she said, and we went back into the pool.

I tried to tell myself it was too hot to be out of the water anyway, and my friend said the suspension felt good on her body, but I was mad at myself that I let my pregnant pal get bullied out of a lounge chair. Still, I figured the only way I could make it worse was if I let the agida ruin our day. So I put it behind me and yapped away with my bestie.

We are champion yappers.

The woman, meanwhile, lay there for hours, without a towel, without a book, squinting at her phone. I sincerely believe she hung out longer than was pleasurable in order to prove how much she needed that chair.

But maybe that just made me feel better.

Despite the early drama, we actually had a great afternoon. When we were ready to get out and go home, I took one last look at the bed in question.

A new person was lying out on it.

All the stress the sun had eased out of me came rushing back in a wave.

Thanks for letting us know.

ADULT TOYS

LISA

Mommy got a new adult toy.

No, not that one.

I had that one already.

Please.

How long have we known each other?

Anyway, I don't even bother anymore.

Who cares?

But I digress, before I even get started.

I'm talking about two other toys.

By the way, I'm making an exception to my usual rule not to talk about products, because the only product I endorse is my books. But if you're not reading my novels by now, I don't know what to say.

I don't want to inflict guilt on you, even though I learned how from the master, Mother Mary.

She raised guilt-infliction to an art form.

When I did something she didn't like, she would say, "You're going to be sorry after I'm dead."

And with that, she would pull out a kitchen drawer and slam it closed.

God knows why she did that with the drawer.

It was punctuation, South-Philly style.

But it did the trick, and in the end, she was right.

Mom, I'm sorry.

I'm sorry for what I did or didn't do.

Most of all, I'm sorry we had kitchen drawers.

That said, I'm in love with a kitchen gadget.

I will explain.

As you may know, I live a quiet life of reading, writing, and wrangling disobedient pets. My food routines include salad, spaghetti, and chocolate cake.

Not in order of preference.

And every morning I have a hard-boiled egg on toast with a slice of avocado or tomato.

So I have to peel a hard-boiled egg.

Can we talk about how freaking annoying it is to peel a hard-boiled egg?

I know, the problem begins with how you boil them in the first place, or how long you cool them, or the barometric pressure of the air in the tristate area, but I don't care.

All I know is my hard-boiled eggs are

impossible to peel.

Every morning, the shells come off in tiny little shards that take forever to peel off. I leave half of them on because I'm too lazy or hungry to bother. Then I wash the egg because dog hair was on my hands, and what I'm trying to tell you is this is way too much devotion to an egg.

Enter the Negg, a gadget that will automatically peel hard-boiled eggs.

My friend Nan is the one who discovered the Negg and she gave it to me as a present.

Thanks, Nan!

The Negg is a little plastic container big enough to fit one egg, and you put water inside to a certain point, then replace the lid and shake the container about six times.

And when you take off the lid, your life changes.

Because the egg is sitting there completely peeled, glistening pure white and ready to be eaten.

I love my Negg.

My day starts with much less profanity, it's fun to shake the container around like a tambourine.

I dance when I do it, but you don't need to.

Now, one caveat.

It doesn't always work so great.

Sometimes it leaves some of the peels on.

And if you shake it too hard, it mashes the egg.

It's not perfect.

But who is?

It's a head start.

And fun in the morning.

Just remember, breakfast is the most important meal of the day.

And the other adult toy is for those of you who have pools.

I know I'm lucky to have a pool, and I use it as much as I can, for a person who doesn't know how to swim and doesn't intend to learn.

But one thing I don't like is that frogs, mice, voles, and once, even a bunny fell inside the pool and drowned.

The first thing I would do every morning is to go out to the pool and save any critters that had fallen in overnight.

I was like a first responder, only too late.

A last responder.

But I got there in time to save some of the critters, though you haven't lived until you've chased a frog around a pool when you're supposed to get to work.

But lo and behold, I heard about a product that addressed this problem.

The Frog Log.

It's a little blue pad that floats in the pool like a polyvinyl island, with a black mesh bridge attached to another cushion anchored outside of the pool.

It's truly a frog bridge, but that didn't rhyme.

I am telling you, it's a great device.

I haven't seen a single critter in the pool in the morning.

And I don't worry anymore.

Happily, all of the vermin remain alive at my house, and I think that's called a happy ending.

Horse Years

LISA

These days, I have a whole new perspective on aging.

Of course, that's exactly what happens when you get older.

You enter this-can't-be-old-because-that's-what-I-am territory.

It's like that song, "When I'm Sixty-Four," plays in a continuous loop in your head.

And you remember when you thought sixty-four sounded old.

And now it's in striking distance.

So it strikes you as young.

I remember not very long ago, everybody was talking about how sixty was the new forty, but now I've passed sixty.

I've set my sights on seventy being the new fifty.

Honestly, it is.

I know seventy-year-olds and they still look and act young to me. They're hiking mountains, riding horses, reading books,

Never too old to have fun with your daughter! (Or to appreciate Lady Gaga.)

and staying current with politics and the arts. When I went to the Lady Gaga concert with Francesca, I expected to be the oldest one there, but the dominant group in the audience were mothers and adult daughters our ages, attending the concert together.

We even sat next to a mother and daughter who read our books.

In other words, our new best friends.

The other thing that's put aging in better perspective for me is animals, in particular, horses.

Just so you have a baseline, a horse isn't

fully grown until he's five years old. That's when his body comes into full maturity.

Don't you wish you could say an age when people come into full maturity?

If you're looking for a horse that you want to ride for fun, five is considered young. The perfect age is about ten or twelve. Before I owned horses, I heard they lived until the age of twenty or sometimes twenty-four, and they could be ridden happily all the time.

Happily, meaning you were happy and they were happy.

Because if you've ever loved an animal, you know that their happiness matters as much as yours.

But what's starting to happen with my horses is they started getting older than I had ever expected, living longer lives happily.

Buddy The Pony is now thirty-two. I ride him all the time and he gets excited when he goes out. He's not retiring anytime soon.

And I have Mr. Fudgie, a quarterhorse rescued from racing, and he just turned thirty-eight years old. Nothing is asked of him these days, except that he look choco-latey good while he eats grass.

He does.

He's basically a high-rent lawn ornament,

Willie looks younger than Lisa, even dozing . . .

and we're both fine with that.

Francesca's horse, Iron Will, is twenty-one years old and completely happy trail riding. I used to think that twenty was old for a horse, now I know it's not.

For horses, twenty is the new ten.

We're all living horse years.

We're living chicken years too.

I have hens that are thirteen and fourteen years old. My chicken vet says they're some of the oldest hens he has ever seen.

So what does all this mean?

To my mind, good news.

You've heard that age is a state of mind,

and while that's true, I'm coming to understand that it's a state of body too.

If we're lucky enough, we're all living longer and living better.

People are working well into their seventies and beyond. If you enjoy what you do, why not?

Life is to be enjoyed, for as long as you can.

And it's guaranteed you're getting better at it, every day.

The other day someone asked me if I think about retiring, and the answer is yes, but I'm not going to do it.

That's the thing I think about retiring.

I don't want to.

By the grace of God, and with the support of wonderful readers like you, I intend to keep writing.

And I intend to keep riding, too.

Nobody at my house is ready to be put out to pasture.

Not while we're so young.

Compare and Contrast

LISA

I've solved The Case of the Missing Eyebrows.

I'm Nancy Drew, post menopause.

We all end up being Nancy Drew, don't we?

We're driving our roadsters through the streets of life, solving mysteries like where we left our cell phone, where we parked our car, or where we put our favorite pair of fleece pants.

You get the idea.

It's all about missing something.

Because we forget.

Some of the missing things matter, so we go looking.

Some of the things don't matter, so we forget about forgetting about it.

And some of the missing things we buy all over again, because we can't remember whether we lost it or never owned it in the first place.

This would be the reason I have four tubs of butter in my refrigerator.

I keep forgetting if I bought it, so I buy it again.

I don't want to run out of butter.

Because I'm on a diet.

I've written before about the fact that my eyebrows are missing, and in response, several wonderful readers wrote me saying that I might have low thyroid levels, or that I'm overplucking.

Thanks for the thoughts, and I love you back.

So do my eyebrows.

I checked my thyroid levels and they're fine, but I didn't bother checking about overplucking.

I can't remember the last time I plucked my eyebrows.

And not because I can't remember, but because it hasn't been in the past thirty years.

I never cared enough about my eyebrows to pluck them.

They looked normal until they vanished.

I've plucked my chin, but never my eyebrows.

And I've plucked my whiskers, because that's not a good look on anybody but a cat.

So we can put those theories to bed.

I found the answer on my own, having cracked the case like the girl detective.

The answer is, science.

Literally.

I did some research and found an article in *Science* magazine.

Did you even know there was a *Science* magazine?

Is there a *Math* magazine?

Do you care?

I subscribe to *People*.

I only like what I'm good at.

Anyway, the article makes clear that disappearing eyebrows are definitely due to age and they're one of the lesser-known signs.

But more precisely, the article says that, "aspects of facial contrast, a measure of how much facial features stand out in the face, decrease with age in women across a variety of ethnic groups."

So that's the villain.

Curse you, facial contrast!

The article said that missing eyebrows were "a cue for perceiving age from the face, even though people are not consciously aware of it."

Bottom line, if your eyebrows are fading away, so are you.

And everybody knows it, you old hag.

Apparently, researchers conducted a study wherein they took pictures of women from four different ethnic groups, then used computer software to generate two versions of the face, one with high contrast and the other with low. People chose the high-contrast face as the young face almost 80 percent of the time.

So there you have it!

At any given time, 80 percent of the people are raising their eyebrows at your missing ones.

The article suggests that "people could actively modify how old they look by altering how much their facial features stand out, for example, by darkening or coloring their features."

So get out your crayons, ladies!

It's not your face, it's a coloring book.

Everybody's dyeing their hair pink and blue, so why not your eyebrows?

You can have blue hair and purple eyebrows and orange lips.

Or why not color one eyebrow red and the other green?

You might look crazy, but at least you'll look young.

You want contrast, *Science*?

We'll give you contrast!

But in truth, I don't think I'll bother.

Eighty percent of the people might dismiss me as a hag, but I'm focusing on the 20 percent who are smarter than that.

The ones who see me, even though I'm fading into the background.

The ones who don't need a blinking neon sign to find a human being.

The ones who value a heart over a face.

And I'm seeing you back.

You'll always count to me, even when others count you out.

Because sometimes, 20 percent can be greater than 80 percent.

That's my kind of math.

THE TRUTH COMES OUT
FRANCESCA

Dating someone new is a delicate dance of introducing yourself as you truly are and guessing at who the other person wants you to be.

I'm good at reading people, sometimes too much for my own good. When I was younger and a guy would approach me, I would size him up and fashion myself in the style of whomever I thought he wanted for the duration of that conversation. It came more from a place of people-pleasing rather than manipulation, but I confess, I thought it prudent to ensure that the guy liked me while I decided whether or not I liked him back. I never outright lied, but I edited the truth.

At a sports bar for my friend's engagement to a guy from upstate, I talked to a future groomsman about my long-suffering Eagles fandom and that I'm a feminist who listens to Howard Stern.

When my older cousin took me to a fundraiser at the posh Union Club, I talked to his friend about what I studied at Harvard and why I prefer Puccini to Wagner.

Both were completely true, if incomplete.

All that game got me was a lot of phone numbers of guys who weren't quite the right match for me. So I've stopped being such a chameleon, and I've worked on being more authentically myself right off the bat.

Never more so with this last guy I dated. We were introduced by mutual friends, and although we had many differences — different nationalities, religions, native languages — we hit it off. I hadn't been so excited about a guy in a long while. And as much as I feared bursting our bubble of infatuation, I forced myself to be honest about my nonnegotiables about who I am and what I'm looking for. Chief among them?

Must love dogs.

I'm genuinely more malleable about religion than I am about my dog, Pip.

Dog is God spelled backwards for a reason.

Of course I love my cat, too, she's not going anywhere, but the dog is my world, and I will always have pets. I communicated this loud and clear on our first date.

He assured me he was right there with me.

"My last serious girlfriend had a rescued pit bull, and that dog loved me more than it loved her."

I had my doubts about that — I remembered how Pip would greet my old boyfriends with such enthusiasm before turning ice-cold the moment we broke up — but I liked his positivity around dog ownership. We were in the clear.

The morning after the first night he spent at my place, we were sitting in my bed talking, and Pip put his paws up on the side of the bed. I felt sorry for relegating him to the floor overnight, so I pulled him up onto my lap.

"Whoa." My new beau recoiled. "I told you I was a dog lover, but I have my limits."

"Is one of those limits dogs on the bed?" I asked with a grin.

He nodded.

"Well, that's too bad, because that's not the rule in this house!"

He laughed and I thought we were cool.

But even so, I put Pip back down on the floor, pretending to be the type of person who only lets her dog on the bed for a momentary snuggle, instead of the truth:

That my date had just spent the night sleeping on "Pip's pillow."

Don't worry, I changed the sheets.

If you come for the king, you best not miss!

Recently.

But I figured this was all part of getting to know each other, and we were basically on the same page. The next several weeks of dating went without incident, until one night, we were walking the dog together before bed. Pip began doing his business on the curb, when all of a sudden, inside my boyfriend's mind, a dam burst.

"You see your dog taking a shit? Think of all the dogs that shit on this sidewalk all day long. This sidewalk is covered in shit. And we wear boots to walk out here, but the dog doesn't. We take our boots off in your apartment, but that dog tracks that shit in your house. And then on you" — he then pantomimed paws by walking his hands up my chest and then pushing them onto my face — "and you *let that dog in your bed*!"

Shocked, I stood still as stone, like a statue holding a plastic baggie. He had rarely cursed or raised his voice before this outburst, and the last time he'd seen the dog in the bed was weeks ago. Had he been stewing on this all that time?

I was angry, but I didn't want to escalate things, so I answered softly, "Well, I love 'that dog,' so I guess I don't mind."

He laughed, and shouted, "You can love him all right, but *that f*cking dog* is tracking shit in your house!"

Dear reader, I can only attempt to convey to you the ice that formed around my heart at that moment: if you had been there, you could've heard the crystals crackle and squeak. I've never tolerated the use of expletives in arguments with boyfriends, certainly not in reference to my son.

I remained calm and replied in a tone that lowered the temperature around me ten degrees, "Don't talk to me like that."

Don't talk to *us* like that.

He rolled his eyes. "C'mon, I can't make a joke?"

"You're joking?" As I heard it, he was telling the truth.

"Oh, okay, fine. You refuse to laugh at any of my jokes tonight." His words still had edge, but his laugh was shot through with nerves. He knew he'd messed up.

I offered the world's tightest smile in case there was any doubt.

We walked back to my apartment in silence. When we got in, I went to get a glass of water because the fury had made my

Pip on "his" Pillow

mouth dry.

When I returned, I found my soon-to-be-ex had, in an act of great optimism or denial, stretched out on my bed.

I took a sip of water. "We need to talk."

See, my truth is, I'm the type of person who will break up with you if you talk about my dog like that, and I couldn't pretend otherwise. I said what followed with more maturity and tact, but the subtext was:

I'm sorry, but I don't let pieces of shit in my bed.

ITCHY AND SCRATCHY, THE SEQUEL

LISA

You may remember that I used to write about Mother Mary's love of backscratchers.

Yes, I made fun of my mother for profit.

You know what?

She approved.

She loved that I wrote about her. In fact, sometimes when I would call her, she would begin the conversation with, "I did something you should write about."

And thanks to all of you, who gave me the chance to give her the spotlight that she deserved, and frankly that all of us deserve.

We all do things that we should write about.

So here I am, writing about them, so you don't have to.

Don't worry, I'm a professional.

I got this.

Today I'm remembering that Mother Mary had six backscratchers in her house.

She even traveled with one when she came to see me, because I didn't have any.

Let me tell you, a backscratcher looks strange in a suitcase.

Actually a backscratcher looks strange anywhere.

A stick with a hand on the end is the stuff of nightmares.

My mother had a backscratcher that was black enamel bamboo and at one end was a realistic hand with long fake fingernails.

Eew.

Still I wish I had that now, but I suspect my brother does. That would be a Scottoline-style family heirloom.

A backscratcher and maybe a pack of matches.

In any event, I got to thinking about my mother and her backscratchers because all of a sudden, my back is superitchy.

I have a backscratcher, but I have to buy about three hundred more. My one is always upstairs, because I keep it under my pillow at night.

How sexy is that?

You know you're in trouble when the adult toy you use the most in the bedroom is a backscratcher.

Or maybe you're not in trouble.

Maybe you're doing just fine.

Maybe you're living your life exactly as God intended, in purity.

But when I'm downstairs without the backscratcher, I find myself rubbing my back on doorjambs like a deer.

I improvise with serving forks, carving forks, and chef's knives.

There isn't a sharp object in the tristate area that I haven't used to scratch my back.

One time I was with Francesca, I asked her to scratch my back, and she did, but the relief was only temporary.

Asking someone to scratch your back never works out the way you hoped.

It takes too long for them to find the itch, since you can't properly direct them.

Saying "there, not there," and "here, not here," isn't very helpful.

And before long, the guilt feels worse than the itching.

And even if they find the itch, they never scratch it long enough.

They get bored, probably because it took so long to find the itch in the first place.

I, however, am just warming up.

Scratching my back all day would do just fine.

But I get it, you have a life.

My back started itching when I turned sixty, and I wondered if it was related to aging, like if my skin is drying up in general.

But if that's true, why don't my legs itch?

Or my arms?

Or my breasts?

I can't tell you the last time I had any feelings whatsoever in my breasts.

So I don't think it's aging.

And so here I am, in dire need of more backscratchers, and on my last book tour, you know what I packed in my suitcase.

Yes, I did.

So it's come full circle, Mother Mary and me, front to back, and back again.

And every time I reach for a backscratcher, I know Mother Mary is laughing her ass off, in heaven.

I've become my mother, but without the smoking.

Profanity included.

You remember at the end of the movie *Carrie,* when the hand reaches up out of the grave?

Well, in the movie *Lisa,* it's Mother Mary who's making my back itch from beyond the grave, and the thing that's sticking up out of the soil is a backscratcher.

It's payback, since I made fun of her all those times.

Or her saying, "I did something you should write about."

And so I am.
Thanks, Mom.

Slip Sliding Away

LISA

Have you seen the commercial for the Sock Slider?

I'm so there.

It's a device that helps people put on their socks and it's intended for people with arthritis or mobility issues.

But what about lazy people like me?

I might order one.

Or maybe two, one for each foot.

And think of the other possibilities.

There could be a Shirt Slider for people who can't lift up their arms, or those like me who simply don't want to.

Or a Pants Slider that holds your pants open while you jump in.

A Bra Slider for those who need help putting on a bra.

Or a Braless Slider for those who realize that bras are optional.

I'll buy that.

I'll take all the help I can get.

Why not?

I say this because last book tour, I brought dresses with zippers on the back and I couldn't zip them up. No matter how hard I tried, I couldn't reach my arm around for the last third of the zip. I was going crazy in my hotel room, whirling around with my elbow in the air.

What's a girl to do?

I couldn't go to my signing that way, so I stopped at a Starbucks and asked a female barista to zip me up.

That's me, no pride.

It's my new Starbucks order.

I'll have a venti iced green tea latte, soy milk, no syrup, and do you mind dressing me?

Nobody minded.

One female barista said with a smile, "I do that for my mom, too!"

I left her a big tip.

I love good daughters.

Of course I didn't ask any of the male baristas, for fear of sexually arousing them.

I'm considerate that way.

So I need a Zipper Slider.

And an Earring Slider.

I can't put my earrings on anymore.

I don't know when this started happening, but I've noticed it recently. If I have an earring with a post, I can't hold the little back and put on the earring. I keep dropping the little back. And the last time I tried, I stabbed myself in the earlobe so hard I practically repierced my ear.

I have the same problem with hoops, where I can't get the gold wire in the little tunnel.

When did everything get so little?

And why don't my fingers work anymore?

In truth, more and more, I can't do any of the fasteners on my jewelry.

I need a Jewelry Slider.

I have one really pretty necklace that I can't fasten in the back.

I can't work any of the catches on any chains at all.

At this point, I wear only necklaces that I can put over my head like a noose.

Lovely.

I'm not sure what the cause of this is. The obvious answer is that it's a getting-older thing, in that as we age, we lose fine motor coordination.

I'm not a doctor, I don't know if that's the answer.

I'm just a lady telling you what's happening from the front line, since I wish somebody had told it to me.

Because I would've bought jewelry with

fewer fasteners.

And if it is about aging, God knows what fresh hell is next.

Before you know it, I'll need a contraption that holds my necklace up in the air, like a basketball hoop for hags.

Then I can scoot underneath and launch myself up into it.

And how long am I going to be able to scoot for?

When do we start rolling me under the necklace and having a machine lower it around my neck?

But I don't know if it's truly about aging.

Because an equal possibility to me is that we start caring less, about dumb things like wearing jewelry.

I remember when it was important to me to wear nice earrings and a necklace. It gave me a lot of pleasure, but I also didn't feel dressed without it.

Now I do.

Now I don't care.

That's the truth about getting older.

The trappings fall away, and everything becomes simpler.

I feel dressed just by waking up in the morning.

Look, world, I get another day of breathing in and out.

Can you beat that for perfect?

A STAN IS BORN
FRANCESCA

My heart raced, my pupils dilated, oxytocin and adrenaline surged through my veins.

Was I on drugs, in love, in bed?

I was at a Lady Gaga concert.

A stan is born.

A "stan" is defined as an overzealous or obsessive fan, it can also be used as a verb, as in, "We stan for a living legend," meaning worship and proselytize. For me with Gaga, it was stan at first sight.

Funny thing was, I'd been dreading that concert before we went. I'd never seen Lady Gaga live before, and I had only a passing appreciation of her music over the years, but I liked her last album especially and dug her Super Bowl performance, so on a whim, I'd splurged on tickets to her outdoor Citi-Field show. When the date came, I miserably watched it rain all day with no sign of stopping. My expensive floor tickets were close to the stage — and far from any overhead covering. And to cap it all off, I'd invited my best friend, who happened to be six months pregnant.

The thought of dragging her out in the rain made me feel terrible. I told her she was free to bail.

"Dude I BOUGHT A PONCHO for this!" she texted back.

This is why we're friends.

So we dressed like the Gorton's fisherman and hoped for the best.

I didn't know the best could be so good.

I'm not going to go on and on about how amazing Gaga was that night, because we can only fit so many pages in this book, and you have your own music taste. All I can tell you is I felt myself change on a molecular level. I was suffused with joy and energy. I was high off it. And not just high, I was attached.

We didn't merely enjoy her performance, we were *converted.*

"Did we just join a cult?" I asked my friend when it was over.

Based on the amount of merch we bought, I think so.

We couldn't stop talking about how incredible she'd been on the long train ride home. I got in after 1:00 A.M., but couldn't sleep. I stayed up, reviewing the photos and videos I'd taken during the concert, reliving every moment. Then I read strangers' tweets about the concert I had just been to. I had to see if anyone else had a religious experience like I had.

Had they ever.

And that was how I got introduced into the Gaga stan community, #LittleMonsters.

Seeing video clips of her current tour in other cities with different stage setups and different adlibs filled me with intense FOMO, and made me wonder:

Should I see her concert again? I mean, it's probably mostly the same show, and tickets aren't cheap. That would be crazy.

I saw her again in Philly with my mom the next week. I said it was to celebrate my mom finishing her book, but that was a cover story, I just wanted to see Gaga again, and it was totally worth it.

Plus I successfully converted my mother, so now we're a Little Monster family.

If I had more time and money, I would Dead-Head Gaga all over the globe.

Instead, I'll have to settle for the virtual proxy of online content. And I've been insatiable.

Fandom is like a snowball and the Internet is the hill. The Internet provides so much material your obsession gains momentum.

I've spent hours in YouTube rabbit holes of Gaga's performance videos — the current tour in different cities, at different angles, past shows, music videos, TV appearances, interviews — and I only fall deeper in love. I can't believe I didn't start stanning for her sooner, I'm making up for lost time.

I could barely write this because I keep taking breaks to watch more YouTube Gaga videos and calling it "research."

I discovered the world of stan-Instagram, accounts devoted solely to posting pictures and clips of Lady Gaga through the years.

In reading all the comments on social media, I've picked up on the special vernacular fans, like a stan-dialect. It's ultrasincere, hyperbolic, and devotional.

"She is such a special human being."

"I love you so much, you are everything to me."

"I wish I could protect her."

"OMG, her laugh is adorable."

And I find myself spontaneously adopting it.

The only lingo I cannot get into is the "Mother Monster" nickname for Lady Gaga. I am Gaga's age exactly (we were born a month apart, yes, of course I know her birthday), so I can't call her Mommy.

But I will totally do the "paws up" hands.

In fact, I'm doing it right now.

Alone, in my apartment.

Don't judge.

I try to resist the martyr language, "Gaga suffers for us!" but even that's hard.

Because she does.

Did you know Lady Gaga has fibromyalgia and suffers from chronic pain? Her fans do. We're very worried.

There was a Netflix documentary about it recently. I've watched it three times. Twice the day it came out.

Did you know Gaga once broke her hip while performing onstage? She sang and danced through the rest of the show, that's how much she loves her fans. You can see it on YouTube.

A comment beneath the video says, "I almost cried just thinking about how much pain she was in but kept going."

Standom is a lot like teenage puppy love. It's all-consuming, unrequited, and chaste. I have a crush, in the purest sense.

Which is why I'm sort of too old for it. It's acceptable for an adult to be a long-term fan of an artist you discovered much earlier, but I don't know if we're supposed to collect any new objects of obsession in our thirties. I think now I'm supposed to appreciate artists instead of stan for them.

Oops.

I *know* I'm too old for this, because one of the Gaga-stan accounts that I follow captioned a gif of Gaga swooning, "I fainted in English class today."

Not English lecture.

English *class*.

This stan is in high school.

And the other funny thing? I was genuinely concerned for this fainting person. Fandom is a family, and because I am probably close to his or her mother's age, I worry about the little sister- and brother-stans.

"Aw, I hope you're feeling better now," I wrote to this stranger.

"Thank you so much!" he or she replied.

It was honestly one of the nicest experiences I've had with a stranger online in months.

People online make snap decisions to hate someone they don't know all the time. It was nice to make a snap decision to love someone.

So beside my computer I taped up a photo of Lady Gaga singing on top of her piano in the pouring rain.

Because I may not have a school locker anymore, but I have rain.

When the standom hits: Gaga-induced euphoria in the pouring rain.

The snark and the cynicism of adulthood gets old faster than we do. Life benefits from an object of admiration, inspiration, geeky enthusiasm, and straight-up joy.

Maybe that's why even grown-ups, especially grown-ups, can use a little standom in our lives.

A Convenient Truth
LISA

I have wonderful news.

Wawa is now offering home delivery.

This is great for locals, who know what Wawa is.

Wawa is a convenience store that we all spent too much time in.

And now, it's becoming even more convenient.

Wawa is offering home delivery through a service called Grubhub.

If you don't go to Wawa, you probably go to another convenience store, and I'm betting that soon your convenience store will offer home delivery, too.

In fact, I just saw online that 7-Eleven offers home delivery through a service called Door Dash.

I don't know the difference between Grubhub and Door Dash, but that doesn't matter. The bottom line is that they're messenger services for food, which is probably the best message anyone ever gets.

Wawa sells ice cream, candy, soft pretzels, and every other carbohydrate on the planet. It will also make sandwiches just the way you like them, let's say a provolone hoagie with sweet pickles, tomatoes, lettuce, mayonnaise and oil, hold the onions.

Hypothetically speaking.

Because evidently, convenient stores weren't convenient enough.

Not for us Americans.

We're either superlazy or superbusy, but either way, I'm fine with it.

I would be delighted to call Wawa, order a cheese hoagie, and have someone bring it to me. I'm also hoping they'll actually feed it to me, so I don't have to hold it myself.

Because that's a lot of work.

And I'm too busy and/or too lazy to do that.

Likewise, I would love some plain potato chips or maybe sour cream and chive chips, which taste delicious.

Maybe I'll order those both, and somebody will bring them to me at my house, open the bags for me, and place several chips in my mouth at a time.

Do you know how they say "you never can have just one"?

I never eat just one at a time.

I stick my hand in the bag, fill it up, and stuff as many chips as possible in my mouth.

I'm hoping that whoever they send over can do that for me and will know that's what I want.

I don't want to have to explain that to them.

Because I am too busy and/or lazy.

I think it might also be difficult for me to have to chew my own food, so I'm hoping that whoever they send over can put one hand on my head and the other on my chin and make my jaw go up and down.

I will take care of the swallowing.

That will be my exercise for the day.

I'm pretty sure I can fit that into my schedule.

It's not as convenient as if somebody else swallowed for me, but that's the type of rugged individualism and can-do attitude that built this country, so I'll try to do it on my own.

Although as a matter of fact, I wasn't around when the country was built, nor were any of my relatives. We were in rural Italy, sitting around a table, having to spoon carbohydrates into our own mouths.

Thank God we left that all behind.

I saw another story online that said 7-Eleven was going to join forces with

Flirtey, which is a drone delivery service.

Now we're talking.

Why waste time with cars and trucks when you can fly?

Can you imagine looking up, and saying, It's a bird, it's a plane, no, it's a bag of chips?

Could there be a better use of drones?

Why deliver bombs when you can deliver sugar bombs?

Flying ice cream, flying popcorn, flying hoagies!

It's a brave New World, my friends,

Who needs to see the sky?

It's blue.

We get it.

Wouldn't you rather look up and see cotton candy instead of clouds?

Tomorrow will be sunny with a chance of beef jerky.

Think how convenient it will be!

Next we'll start flying the foods into our mouths.

I'm pretty sure this is why my grandparents came over on the ship.

They heard the streets were paved with drones.

SNAKES ALIVE

LISA

It was going to happen, sooner or later.

I found a snake in the family room.

Let me give you some background.

You may remember the story of the day I came home from food shopping and found snakes writhing in a massive ball on my front walk.

Yes, that really happened.

Francesca thought it was really cool and filmed the whole thing with her phone.

I didn't think it was cool and ran inside the house screaming.

Which is when I learned it was apparently mating day for all of the snakes in the tristate area, who had gathered at my house for an orgy.

That happened about two years ago, and ever since then I've been noticing snakes here and there, where they shouldn't be.

Actually, snakes shouldn't be anywhere, but I guess they have a right to live even though they're vermin.

Like politicians.

So occasionally I'll find a snake in the garden, or one by the fence gate, resting in the sun.

But I never thought I'd find one in the house.

Until today.

I was getting a book in the family room and happened to notice something curled in the corner.

It looked like a short piece of dark string, which was strange, but not that strange.

My house is never that clean.

You never know what you'll find in the corner.

Usually it's a dust bunny, mound of dog hair, or toenails from the cat.

Does your cat leave toenails everywhere?

I swear, not a day goes by that I don't find a cat toenail embedded in the rug, lying on the floor, or stuck in a cushion.

My couch has more toenails than my cat.

And that's why I wasn't unduly alarmed when I saw a random piece of string in the corner.

When I went over, it moved.

And then I was alarmed.

It was a baby snake.

In fact, its babyness was the only thing

that kept me from freaking out completely.

This, because I spend way too much time online, looking at pictures of baby animals of all kinds, including reptiles, frogs, and octopuses.

If you're on those sites, you know what I'm talking about.

They're called cute overload, or land of cute, or beyond cuteness, and you get the general idea.

Baby things are cute.

And surprisingly, even snakes.

It just looked up at me with its dark eyes, then it opened its mouth and its little red tongue came out.

Cute, right?

The snake didn't try to move away or anything. It was evidently too young to be afraid of me, and I told myself that I was too old to be afraid of it.

We stood there looking at each other, neither of us knowing what to do.

I had enough time to run back to the kitchen, get a pot, and return to the snake and set it down.

"Jump in!" I said in a friendly way.

The snake looked at the pot, and I gave it a little push from behind, and it slithered inside the pot.

So I taught it a trick!

And of course I wouldn't kill it, so I brought it outside to the backyard, far away from the house, and set it free.

I assumed it had gotten inside the house because there's a set of French doors off the family room, which I may have left open.

I got back to the house feeling terrific about myself, the baby snake, and the world in general until I realized something.

I had no idea if it had a mother, left inside.

Or a father.

Or a sister or brother.

You know, a ssssibling.

Was its whole family in my family room?

So you know I tore that room up.

I looked under every couch, every chair, every cushion, every rug corner, and behind all of the books, just in case.

But I didn't find any more snakes.

Which was good news and bad news.

What if they're upstairs in my bed?

KEEP IT MOVING

FRANCESCA

I will do everything in my power to avoid the checkout line at the drugstore.

I will refill a prescription a month in advance in order to pay for my items at the pharmacy counter.

I will scan and rescan one item six times at the glitchy self-checkout machine without complaint.

The line at the drugstore changes you.

First, there's an issue of mismanaged expectations. Nobody anticipates a long wait at the front. At the pharmacy, sure — that guy's rash demands answers. But at the main checkout, when you're holding only some floss and a pack of toilet paper, you expect a quick errand.

A fool's errand.

When you begin to realize it's taking awhile, you question yourself. Why are you even buying this floss anyway? You're going to use it for two days and then forget forever. But you need the toilet paper, bad, you've already gone through the Kleenex box, so you have to wait in the line.

And wait.

And wait some more.

The store can seem completely empty while you're shopping, but the line is always full. There could be only three people ahead of you, but it counts as full because there's only one person working among the many, empty registers.

It's like an optical illusion of service.

Every drugstore has a giant counter of five or six registers at checkout, but have you ever seen more than one cashier working at them?

Okay, *two* cashiers maybe, but the second appears only after the first makes several pleas over the intercom, and the new one always seems low-key angry about it.

So you've got a pinch-hitter cashier who's mad she got interrupted from staring down teens at the condom section, and the original cashier who's mad she had to call twice, and a line of irritated customers wondering why she took so long, and why the guy in front of them is taking so long, and before you know it, the whole place is rife with low-simmering resentment.

As a child of divorce, I both hate it and

feel very at home.

I was really sweating it last time because I intended to commit a cardinal sin.

I wanted to use coupons.

Gotta love those sweet, sweet rewards.

People complain about the long receipts, but come on. Those receipts contain coupons for *cash back.*

I wish more stores would inconveniently give me money.

That day, I needed razor-blade refills and deodorant, and I was going to use a coupon for the razors to get cash back to use on the deodorant, which happened to have an in-store discount as well. It was the kind of convoluted coupon shenanigans I knew would paint a target on my back in rewards-bucks red.

"I'd like to buy this stuff in two separate transactions, please," I said at the register.

Someone behind me gave a loud sigh.

But the deodorant discount didn't show up. I pointed out the omission to the clerk.

"That offer doesn't apply to the twin packs," she said.

"Really? Because it said on the shelf *any* Dove product more than eight dollars qualified."

"Then that deal is expired."

It seemed like she was making up reasons.

I was having an internal battle between my people-pleasing tendencies and the hardening effect of being in the line.

"Would you mind checking?"

She called for a manager. I couldn't turn around to see if anyone was coming because I was too afraid to face my fellow customers' wrath. But I could hear them.

"All this hold up for one person?" one griped.

Mercifully, the manager arrived quickly. She tried it again on the register and shrugged to her colleague. "If it's listed, you have to give it to her." Then she looked at me. "Can you show me?"

Did she know what she was asking me? The line would kill me for this.

I practically ran to the aisle. I showed her the discount posting, clearly valid and applicable, so I returned victorious.

"Okay, with the two offers combined, you saved four dollars today."

"That's it?" said the voice behind me.

"Great, thank you," I said to the clerk. "I appreciate the trouble, and sorry for the wai—" I'd turned to apologize to the line, expecting a pile up of angry customers, but trailed off when I saw there was only one: a little old lady scowling at me.

"I'll say. You took forever!"

I was shocked that all that huffing and puffing had come from this tiny person. In any other context you'd want to help her across the street. Now I was backing away slowly.

On my way out, I did overhear what she was doing at checkout.

She was returning a tube of toothpaste.

Hoodie Eyes

LISA

Time to confess.

I have hooded eyes.

Do you even know what that is?

If you want to see a picture of hooded eyes, look at my author photo.

My hooded eyes are right underneath my disappearing eyebrows.

In other words, take a look at my author photo and try to imagine where my eyebrows would be if I still looked like a human being.

Then try to find my eyelid, but that's a trick question.

I have hooded eyes, so you can't find my eyelid.

I can't either, so the joke's on me.

Here is the nonmedical definition of hooded eyes:

When you get to be a hag, gravity takes over your body and everything lowers. Every part of you sags, including the skin over your eyes, which drapes over your eyelid so far that it doesn't look like you have an eyelid anymore.

That would be the definition, from the trenches.

I looked online to try to define hooded eyes, and of course there is no medical definition, but there are plenty of definitions according to L'Oréal and other makeup companies.

Which view hooded eyes as a situation to be remedied *tout de suite.*

According to the L'Oréal website, "Well, when you have hooded eyes, that means the crease created by your eyelid can appear to be hidden."

They started with "Well," to let you down easy.

Unlike gravity, that bitch.

They could've said, "Well, when you get to be a hag . . ."

But they didn't.

In case you don't know your own age.

Or have yet to accept your hagdom.

They also could've said, "You want to know what hooded eyes are? Well, are you sitting down?"

Of course you're sitting down.

Because you're a hag.

That's what we do.

By the way, I was only forty years old when I got my eye hoods.

That was twenty years before I entered haghood.

I'm looking forward to the next stage of life, when I become a crone.

I think it will be a lot of fun, and you can be one of my cronies.

According to L'Oréal's Makeup Tutorial for Hooded Eyes: "When this occurs, certain eye makeup looks aren't as easily visible since the eyelid appears to be smaller."

This would be the understatement of the year.

Put simply, you can't see your eyeliner if it's hiding under your saggy-ass eye skin.

I started on this topic because I was fine with my hooded eyes this morning, when I noticed that my eyelids are now drooping so low that they're resting on my eyelashes.

If you ask me, that's slacking, even for slack skin.

In fact, my eyelid is actually bumpy because it's following the line of my eyelashes, and my eyelashes don't have the strength to hold up my eyelid, so they're tilting down.

I know, sounds superhot doesn't it?

It makes me look permanently sleepy, which come to think of it, isn't far from the truth.

Lucky for us hags, L'Oréal website has "makeup tips and tricks for hooded eyes" which "you can master to give the appearance of a larger, happier, wide awake set of eyes."

This is asking a lot from a pair of eyes, in my opinion.

I can see.

That's really all I ask from my eyes.

Even though I wear glasses and/or contacts, I'm still not mad at my eyes.

They're still doing their job.

Now, they have to be happy?

A lot of people aren't happy at their job.

But they show up for work every day.

My eyes are professional.

Meanwhile, I've heard of hungry eyes, but never happy eyes.

And I'm not sure that hooded eyes look unhappy.

But I don't think I could convince L'Oréal of it. One of the makeup tips is, "flick a little eyeliner up at the edges for instantly revived winged cat eye."

Wait, what?

Now we have cat eyes?

Happy cat eyes or sad cat eyes?

Large cat eyes or little cat eyes?

Hooded cat eyes or cat eyes without the hood?

Listen, I will tell you the truth.

Because I'm not trying to sell you makeup.

There is no high-priced shadow, liner, or spackle you can throw on your eyelids that will correct or minimize hooded eyes.

Because you can't see it anymore.

So don't bother.

Just consider yourself lucky that you don't have to use eyeliner anymore, much less the liquid eyeliner that makes cat eyes.

Because that was hard to do.

Anytime I used liquid eyeliner, it looked like somebody's EKG.

So now I don't have to bother.

I'm embracing my hooded eyes.

In fact, I'm going to call them hoodie eyes.

Just to remind myself how much fun they are.

See you later.

SUCKING UP

LISA

I just read a news story about a man who thought he had a lung tumor.

But it turned out to be a toy he'd inhaled as a child.

This is an absolutely true story.

Actually, all of the stories in this book are true, but most of them are bizarre things that happened to me.

This is a bizarre thing that happened to somebody else.

It turns out that there was a postal worker in Britain who had been treated for a bad cough, and an X-ray revealed a mysterious mass in one of his lungs. The doctor thought it was a tumor, performed a bronchoscopy, and found a tiny toy cone from a Playmobil set.

Which the man remembered getting for his seventh birthday, forty years before.

Wow.

The doctors took out the cone, and the

man's cough disappeared.

Plus he got his toy back.

Do endings get any happier than that?

Or harder to believe?

He couldn't remember eating the toy cone, but obviously, he must have.

I have that problem too.

I never remember the things I eat.

I could swear I'm not eating anything, but mysteriously, I just gained five pounds.

I must have eaten the entire Playmobil dollhouse.

And the dolls.

Plus the play and the mobil.

It was also incredible that the toy cone didn't go into his stomach, but into his lungs.

That's another problem I have.

Anything I eat goes into my hips.

But the story got me thinking about random toys I could've eaten at that age.

Barbie comes immediately to mind.

As in, Barbie shoes.

You remember Barbie shoes, don't you?

They were plastic high heels that came in different colors and never stayed on her foot.

Maybe because she was permanently on tiptoe.

Or maybe because high heels aren't worth

the trouble.

I loved everything about Barbie, but I was fixated on her shoes, which I collected and sorted by color.

I took better care of Barbie's shoes than I do of my own.

And weirder than that, I also had a habit as a child of walking around on tiptoe.

Like, all the time.

I remember my mother and father being concerned about it and even taking me to a doctor.

Which was so not the Scottoline way.

We never went to doctors because Mother Mary believed in the healing powers of Vicks VapoRub.

I'm surprised she didn't rub it into my feet and call it a day.

My entire childhood smelled like camphor and tomato sauce.

Anyway, the doctor said that there are a percentage of kids who are "toe-walkers," that my parents shouldn't worry about it, and I would grow out of it by age five.

He was partly right.

They shouldn't have worried about it, and they didn't, after that.

But I never grew out of it.

I still do it, even today.

Not all of the time, but sometimes.

Weirded out yet?

I never even realized I do it until I was speaking at a book signing and people started asking me why I was standing on tiptoe. And I realized that I speak on tiptoe at most of my signings, and I'm the most comfortable that way.

I looked it up online and it says that there are adults who toe-walk and that it doesn't indicate an underlying neurological problem.

Obviously they don't know me that well.

The articles say that it can mean your Achilles tendon is too short, but I don't know how long my Achilles tendon is, and in any event, I'm short too, so my Achilles tendon probably matches me.

Otherwise how would it fit in wherever it is?

You can see I'm no biologist.

Online it says that adult toe-walkers with an unknown cause are called idiopathic toe-walkers.

There's no need for name-calling, Internet.

In any event, I don't know why I do it.

Maybe to feel taller.

Or maybe in my mind, I'm wearing Barbie shoes.

At least I'm not eating them.

The Perfect Dump
FRANCESCA

Everyone has hidden talent, mine is the perfect dump.

Wait, that sounds bad. What I mean is, I'm great at breaking up with someone. I can end a relationship tactfully and completely, no mess, no drama, no hard feelings. It's my magic power. I am a breakup ninja.

By the end of it, they're not crying, they're thanking me for the privilege of not dating me.

Need proof? Let this sink in: none of my exes have a harsh word to say about me, and *I write about them for a living.*

Was I born with this knowledge? No. I learned, and so can you.

I cut my teeth in the breakup field by getting dumped myself, a lot. My first boyfriend and I dated from junior year of high school until sophomore year of college. We were on and off the entire time, always at his whim. We imagined grand, grown-up reasons for this *doleur exquise,* but the cause was likely more juvenile: he was afraid of feelings and I was an overachiever who could not accept defeat. So our relationship was like the *Groundhog Day* of having my heart broken. When I'd finally had enough, I understood the meaning of life *and* the most painless way to be dumped.

I'm not ashamed of getting dumped, in fact, I prefer it. Breaking up with someone is excruciating. I hate hurting people's feelings, that's why I learned how to minimize it. My breakup skills are renowned among my friends; they frequently enlist me to rehearse their breakup talks and draft gentle let-down text messages, and I'm happy to help. All may be fair in love and war, but we should do our best to limit the casualties.

Here are my rules for the perfect dump:

1. *Telegraph your intent.* This tip is counterintuitive but key. Surprise is not your friend when breaking up with someone. Getting dumped already feels like being blindsided, receiving a "can we talk?" text affords your partner some crucial mental prep, so they'll feel more composed and dignified during the

discussion. Just don't give *too much* advance notice; you don't want the axe hanging over their head for a full week. But a half day of lead time is perfect. Your partner will take that time to preemptively go through the stages of relationship-grief, and ideally you'll catch them somewhere between depression and acceptance. By the time you actually dump them, they will have already decided you suck, and the talk will be quick and painless for both of you.

2. *Location, location, location.* This depends on the duration and intensity of the relationship. For a long-term relationship with a person you trust and know to be safe, I recommend a private place where you can both cry and snot at will, i.e., one of your homes. For less serious couples, the common wisdom is a public place is best, but all public places are not created equal. Choose somewhere not too busy or cramped, where people mind their own business, and it's easy to hear each other: a café, a wine bar on a weeknight, or a public park.

3. *Whatever you do, don't order food.* Now is not the time to let your unwitting partner order a three-course meal. You know what makes someone lose their appetite? Hearing that their partner is tired of having sex with them. Choose a café or bar with a minimal menu and just get something to drink, or choose an hour where it's clear that we're only doing a snack. If you're breaking up with someone anywhere that has table service, you need to wait to start the breakup conversation until after your order has been taken, so that your rehearsed monologue isn't interrupted by a server, and so no one has to peruse a menu through tears. I hope it goes without saying that the dumper is picking up the check. You'll save money on all the future dates you're not going on.

4. *Go first.* Don't open with, "How do *you* think this is going?" or any question you already know the answer to. This is the coward's opener, born from an irrational hope that your partner will do your dirty work for you. But you cannot assume

they agree with you. If they did, they would be the one dumping you right now. If you pass the ball like this, even if your partner smells trouble, most polite humans will say something nice and optimistic like, "I think it's going pretty well . . ." only to be made a fool of in the next thirty seconds. The time to ask about their feelings is *after* you've offered yours so they have a chance to save face with, "yeah, I was having doubts, too." Who cares if it's the truth? Let them have their dignity, they'll need it to survive all the first dates they're about to endure. You'll know you've done a good job dumping someone when they leave the conversation believing it was a mutual decision.

5. *Omit needless words.* Strunk & White would've dumped with style. Tact doesn't require rambling, so limit yourself to one or two lines of flattery. Anything more is cruel and confusing. It's misdirection at best, and bullshit at worst. To the listener, excessive flattery reads as, "You're so amazing, blah blah blah, but not good enough for me." Once it's

clear where you're headed, get to the point and put them out of their misery. Let the heartbroken ramble and waste time, they're the one in need of patience and generosity, not you.

6. *Judge Judy it.* "The cases are real, the rulings are final." The perfect dump is not a brainstorm or a debate; it's a verdict. You are there to tell someone about a decision you have made. Make it clear that you've given this serious thought (but don't make it sound like you've known it was over and humored them for weeks, that's embarrassing) and now your mind is made up. Do not confuse waffling with empathy. It isn't kinder to feign uncertainty about your decision — all that does is force the dumpee to plead their case or even beg, which is beneath their dignity. They may beg anyway, but it shouldn't be because you misled them into thinking they still had a chance. So apologize, but don't waver. If you still want to be talked out of the decision to break up, then you aren't really ready to have the breakup talk

in the first place.

7. *The Supreme Court Rule.* If you want your ruling to last, your explanation has to be airtight, otherwise you will be mired in litigation. For most dumpees to find the conversation satisfying and closed, you'll have to give them some reason *why.* The best way to do this is to speak about yourself and your subjective feelings as to why the relationship cannot continue, as opposed to offering an analysis of why the other person was a bad partner. "It's not you, it's me," is a breakup cliché because it works. Even if your breakup is highly justified by their shitty behavior, say you got cheated on, it's still better to say, "I don't trust you, so we can't move forward," instead of, "You're a scumbag liar," because in the latter case, you open the door for the person to defend themselves, vow to be different, fight, beg, etc., and before you know it, the conversation has gone on for hours leaving you confused, exhausted, and weak. On the other hand, no one can argue with your feelings, you know yourself

best. It's also the truth. The question at hand isn't whether or not this person is good or bad — who are we to judge? — it's whether or not they're good for you. On that, judge away!

8. *Don't dwell on your mental anguish.* You're thinking, but Francesca, you just told me to talk about my feelings! Yes, but that's your feelings about the relationship, not the breakup itself, and not *ad nauseum.* I often cry when I break up with a guy, not on cue — I wish, I'm not that good of an actress — but because I usually still care for them a lot. That said, I don't go on and on about how hard this is for me, and I try to hold it together as much as possible. When dumping someone, you don't *also* get to be comforted and reassured by the person whose heart you're breaking. Cry to your friends. Excessive agony communicates uncertainty, and that sends you back to Judge Judy.

9. *Take your licks.* No matter how justified you may be in leaving this person, a breakup is emotional, and they're allowed to be mad at you,

even a little petty. If the dumpee starts criticizing you and revising history, it's probably out of hurt and not worth debating. This person is already your ex, and it's honestly advantageous to you both if he or she rationalizes the end of the relationship. Set your ego aside, err on the side of magnanimity, and take it — *within reason.* If the person becomes furious, abusive, or rehashes endlessly, get outta there! Remember, love comes with no guarantees, and you are allowed to break things off for whatever reason, at any time!

10. *Have plans later.* I was once trying to break up with a guy in college after a mere two months of dating, but he somehow embroiled me in a two-hour cry-fest of his recrimination and hysterics. The only thing that saved me from that hell was my best friend calling me and calling me because I wasn't showing up for our dinner plans. In addition to leaving me with a series of the funniest voice mails that I saved for years (example: "Hello, friend. Are you trapped in a cyclone of emotion?"), this taught me an important

lesson. Even the best-laid breakup plans often go awry. Having a good friend who knows what's going on and expects to see you soon is crucial for your safety and sanity.

11. *Always agree to be friends.* Maybe you mean it, maybe you don't, you can both decide that later when things calm down, but it's a nice note to end on.

And that's it! That's everything you need to know to dump like a pro — or at least like a considerate adult. I can't guarantee you a clean break, as there's always that pesky other person in the mix, but you'll know you did your best.

Now, that's settled.

Can anyone teach me how to stay together?

LOWLIGHT

LISA

Cheaters never prosper.

I didn't make that up. Someone else did, and I'm guessing they weren't talking about hair color.

But they should've been.

Where do we begin?

We begin with the story of my hair, the color in particular. I've been coloring my hair for forty years and I forget my natural color.

It hardly matters.

I write fiction for a living.

I see no reason why my hair shouldn't be completely fabricated.

Blond is a lot more fun than mousey-brown reality.

Plus have you seen my author photo lately?

There's not a wrinkle on my face.

I'm a freshly ironed sheet.

As if I never frowned or smiled my entire life.

I look like a virgin.

And that's why God invented Photoshop.

Same with hair color.

Especially when the fictional equivalent of my hair has tawny streaks from a mythical sun over Ventura, California.

Of course I've never ventured to Ventura.

But I'm a California girl.

In my mind.

The term "sun-kissed" is what an ad would say, though a kiss from the sun might be hotter than prudent.

Way back when, I used to put lemon juice on my hair to achieve the desired fake effect, and after that I sprayed some goop called Sun-In, which may have been cleaning solvent mixed with moonshine.

Ironic, since I was aiming for sunshine.

In any event, as I got older, I earned more money and my pretensions grew. I got my hair colored professionally, which they started calling highlighted.

I'm fine with that.

I have great associations with highlights. Yellow markers that we use to overachieve, and also my favorite magazine of all time.

I mean, who doesn't love Goofus and Gallant?

No, I'm not talking about Thing One and Thing Two.

Okay maybe I am, but you're only half-right.

In any event, at some point after highlights, there was something called lowlights, which was supposed to give a more natural look to your fake hair, and I was fine with that too.

I was fine with all this because I have a wonderful haircolorist who I have been going to forever, and she has become my friend, therapist, and general beautifier.

I would never cheat on her. But what happened was that I was on the road, and you know how that goes.

There are men who cheat when they're out of town, but women do too.

But with haircolorists.

What happened was that I had to go to a meeting in New York and I couldn't go with my gray roots, since I'm supposed to look young.

Good luck with that.

I felt like I needed to get blonder and brighter and sunnier, so I went to a haircolorist in New York City.

She was young, adorable, and fun, which is probably how cheaters feel about their girlfriend instead of their wife.

Of course, I felt guilty and more Catholic than ever, since I knew I was cheating.

Even though I had a good excuse, I still felt nervous the whole time I was in the chair.

In fact, people in the electric chair have been more relaxed.

But no shade to her, as the kids say, because I asked her to highlight my hair and she thought I needed more lowlights, and basically what happened is she did exactly what I asked.

Now all of my gray is covered, but I have black roots.

So I don't feel old, I feel slutty.

This is what happens when you cheat, people.

It's a slippery slope.

I love my girlfriend, but I love my wife more.

And I can't wait to get back to her.

It'll be a highlight.

Legalize Pots

LISA

It all started with the garden.

I don't mean that in the biblical way.

As you may know, I really love my garden, which is full of unruly perennials, like black-eyed Susan, phlox, plumbago, coneflowers, hydrangea, Shasta daisies, and false sunflowers, and brush roses.

You get the idea.

It's a mishmash.

I've read a bunch of lovely gardening books that talk about "theme gardens," but my garden has no theme.

The theme is whatever was on sale.

The book suggests you can plant a theme garden with all white flowers, or one that has flowers in superbright colors, or one that has flowers in only muted colors.

I chose all of the above.

And I chose too many flowers.

They've grown and spread out in three years, so they're all running into each other

310

in mass plantings, which is exactly what I wanted, believe it or not.

One of the gardening books called it a cottage garden, which sounded to me like a better name than kitchen-sink garden.

My plan was to get a bunch of flowers, and my only stipulation was that they be perennials, because I will be damned if I will plant this garden every single year.

Maybe a better name is lazy-girl garden?

Anyway I planted it in a designated area in the front lawn above a stone wall and flanking the front walk to my house, and I've really come to love it.

I even built a small garden room so I could work and eat overlooking the garden.

So you would think everything would be fine.

But I admit, I wanted more.

I just wanted more flowers to look at, but I had no room in the garden.

But that didn't stop me from going to the garden center anyway.

True gardeners will know about this addiction.

You don't have room for one more plant, but somehow your car drives you to the garden center, so you can look longingly at plants you should not buy.

And you will buy them.

I feel the same way about books.

I keep buying books and adding book-shelves, then more books and more book-shelves, and the truth is, both of these are addictions I'm proud to have.

Life doesn't get better than books and flowers.

So in one of these jaunts I found myself at the garden center, where I noticed they were having a big sale on pots, 40 percent off and the pots were of all shapes and sizes and colors, like enamel blue, green, and even a soft golden yellow.

I thought, that's not a bad idea.

I have a garden, but I don't have any pots.

Maybe this is a way to expand the garden now that I've run out of real estate.

So I bought three pots, some potting soil, and a new batch of perennials that were called blanketflowers, which were a gorgeous yellow.

I got them home and planted them, and then started putting them on the steps in the garden.

The next day I was working at the table and looking at my pots and thought, I could really use a few more pots.

And I knew the sale was still on at the garden center.

I would've jumped up immediately, but I

hadn't made my word count for the day. For those of you who are interested in the writing process, I write at least two thousand words every day, and I'm not allowed to do any less than that. That's fine with me, and that's generally the length of a chapter in a novel, so I love it. So as soon as I had hit my two-thousand-word count, I went to the garden to get more pots.

Evidently, I have a quota when it comes to words, but not pots.

I bought four more pots, potting soil, and a bunch of bright red coneflowers.

I got them home, planted them, and the next day, when I was writing again at my laptop, I started looking over at my seven pots and thinking.

They're so pretty, but seven is an odd number.

I like even numbers.

And there's plenty of room for more pots.

And that 40 percent sale isn't going to last forever.

And they had so many nice pots left.

Which is when I realized that you can get addicted to pots.

Pots might be a gateway drug.

To more pots.

Because for the next several days, I kept going back and back and back to the garden center, getting more pots, finding more flowers, and planting them like crazy.

I still can't even believe how great it looks.

I ended up with twenty-seven pots.

I know it's an odd number, but I've made peace with it.

At least for the present.

I'm pretty sure I can quit anytime.

DANGEROUSLY POLITE
FRANCESCA

I recently bought some skincare products, and the saleswoman told me I qualified for a free facial. I declined. Beauty and body treatments, ostensibly indulgent and pampering, never seem to go well for me.

I can be dangerously polite.

In my regular life, I'm confident and assertive, but in a salon chair or spa table, I become meek. I never want to seem like a difficult or ungrateful client, I have a baseline of guilt to have another person catering to my needs, so I've bit my lip through blow-dryers that burn my scalp and pedicures that cut me to the quick.

I have had only one professional massage in my life. My mom took me on a Hawaiian vacation as a gift for graduating college, and on one rainy day, we decided to go to the hotel spa and get massages.

Looking at the spa menu, I was overwhelmed by choice. "What's just a regular massage? Swedish?" I asked my mom.

"No, Swedish massage is too hard. Start with something softer."

I chose the "waterfall massage" with "rejuvenating hydrotherapy." I remember my biggest concern was whether or not I should wear a bathing suit.

The room was tiled and dimly lit with a massage bed in the middle of it and multiple showerheads above. The masseuse was sweet and chatty, which I appreciated because it made the fact that I was lying there naked a little less awkward. (They told me to take off the bathing suit.)

I was lying on my back and the masseuse told me that she was going to cover my face with a towel and I should close my eyes and relax. Then I felt the "waterfall" part kick in, as streams of warm water pulsed over my body, and the towel on my face grew heavy and damp.

Is this part of it? I wondered.

Soon the towel was completely soaked, water dripped down my nose and burned the back of my throat, and it was hard to breathe. I tried to turn my head to find a better angle and give a few forceful snorts to clear the water, but no use. Finally I reached up to remove the washcloth from my face.

The masseuse yelped. "Oh my God, I'm *so* sorry! I must have had the showerheads positioned wrong."

Apparently no water was supposed to get on my face at all, the towel was only intended to protect me from splash. She begged me not to complain to the management.

I assured her not to worry about it. I felt way too stupid to admit that I didn't even realize my massage was going wrong until I was basically waterboarded.

I swear, I'm quite good at asserting myself when I have clothes on.

The more intimate the service, the more compliant I become. Think I couldn't get more vulnerable than lying naked on a massage table?

Then let me tell you about the time I got a Brazilian bikini wax.

It was in college. I had never had one before, but my friends told me it was no big deal. One girl who got them regularly told me, "it's the only way I feel clean," which, just, wow. And another said, "It's like having a sexy secret."

I got the idea in my head, because my college boyfriend had casually mentioned that I was the only girl he had ever been with who wasn't completely bare down there.

"It's sexy," he had said, in a valiant attempt to save the moment. "It's like they were girls and you're a real *woman.*"

Not exactly the distinction I craved at age twenty.

So for Valentine's Day, I decided to try it. The waxer did one side, and it hurt as I expected. When she did the second side, I was shocked.

"Oh golly, wow," I said. I don't think I've ever said "golly" aloud before or since. The more curse words that flew through my head, the more quaint my expressions became. Then I *apologized* and made the understatement of the century, "that side hurt a lot more than the first one."

"That happens. Everyone is different," she said before telling me we were all done and quickly exiting the room.

I paid at the front and hobbled across the street to meet my best friend for frozen yogurt.

Fro-yo can make women feel better about anything.

"Hey, how was it?" my friend asked. "Not as bad as you thought, right?"

"It was worse. I can't believe people do this every week."

I tried to console myself with my mango fro, but the pain was distracting. I went to the bathroom to check myself.

I nearly fainted.

My underwear was filled with blood. No amount of toilet tissue could sop it up, I was actively bleeding, a lot.

A sexy secret!

So the first person who saw my Brazilian wax was not my boyfriend but a nurse at the university hospital. She treated me for a "laceration" and said she couldn't be sure whether it was a burn or a tear.

I paid someone to do this to me. Not only that, I tipped 20 percent.

Needless to say, it was not a great Valentine's Day. My boyfriend got my barely contained fury and I got a full course of antibiotics.

Home and fully dressed, I did call the salon to report what had happened. They refunded me and offered a gift certificate as apology.

I said, "No, thank you."

Polite to the last.

Hello, Mom?

LISA

I'd love to tell you a story, but I have to go.

I'm getting a phone call from my dog.

Well, not yet, but I will be any day now.

How?

With Petchatz.

What's that?

The Petchatz HD is a video camera and speaker system that you mount on the wall, hook up to your home Wi-Fi, and download to your phone, which enables you to see and talk to your pet via video.

Arf!

If you want to connect with your dog, you use the app, which plays a ring tone and your dog will come to the video screen.

Arf Arf!

And not only that, you can get other accessories, like a machine that dispenses a treat remotely, so that if your dog comes to the video camera when you call, you can give him a treat.

Arf Arf Arf!

I'm not sure who's being trained here, the dog or the person, but what's the difference?

I love my dogs and I love giving them treats, and I think I might like it even more if I didn't have to put up with their barking for treats in the same room.

In other words, I love my dogs remotely.

Just kidding.

And according to the Petchatz website, you can even "record and share your videos," which opens up new realms of possibilities.

You can record your dog and send the video to your cat.

And you can tag your parakeet and your ferret.

The other accessory is something called the PawCall, whereby your pet can call you on your smartphone.

It's a plastic gadget that sits on the floor, and on top is a big green button in the shape of a pawprint.

And to make a long story short, you're supposed to schedule call times in your app, which causes the green pawprint to blink, and in time, your pet can be trained to call you over Petchatz.

I can't decide if this is idiocy or genius.

The website says Petchatz will alleviate

your pet's boredom and sadness when it's home alone all day.

In other words, the sales pitch is guilt.

I have no problem with that.

Guilt is a great motivator, especially for women.

Nobody wants to be a bad mother.

Even if their child is a hamster.

The website shrewdly exploits this in a banner that says in big letters, YOUR FURBABY IS WAITING FOR YOU TO CALL! ORDER TODAY!

Before we go any further, I confess that I've totally bought into the whole "furbaby" thing.

At first, I resisted.

They're animals, not babies with fur.

But then I stopped being so picky.

They're furbabies because I love them like babies with fur, worry about their physical and emotional needs 24/7, and on top of that, have to prove I'm a terrific mother.

So you know I'm buying this gadget.

Even though I work at home.

I do travel, and I like the whole idea.

The only problem is I can only imagine how phone conversations with my pets will go. As you may know, I have four Cavalier King Charles spaniels, Peach, Little Tony, Boone, and Kit.

If Peach calls, I won't be able to get her off the phone. She'll talk nonstop. I know this because she barks nonstop. She's always at the window, yapping at a squirrel, a blue jay, or a deer.

If she calls me, I'm hitting Decline Call.

Or I might ask Boone to answer the phone and tell her I'm out.

Kit is almost as yappy as Peach, plus he barks at planes. If he called me on the phone, he'd be one of those dogs that starts with, "Did I catch you at a bad time?"

I'd answer, "Yes, Kit, I'm busy working."

To which he'd reply, "Okay, but let me just tell you, there's something flying in the sky that's big and silver and you need to start worrying about it, like I am."

Even dogs don't mean it when they ask if they're calling at a bad time.

They'll bark through your boundaries.

I'm the same way.

I can imagine what Little Tony would do if he could call me. He's the quietest of my dogs, but he's very clingy, so I'm figuring he'd call me a bunch of times a day, but the conversations would be the same:

"Hello, Mom?"

"Hello, Mom?"

"Hello, Mom?"

"Hello, Mom?"

And Boone is food-crazy, so as soon as he realized there could be a treat for a call, he'd call me right away. But I wouldn't be able to understand what he was saying, because his mouth would be full.

Ruby The Incontinent Corgi is my fifth dog, and the only one I would trust with the phone. But corgis tend to be bossy, and she'd call to tell me to bring home milk, bread, and diapers.

And of course there's Vivi, my cat.

Let me ask you this:

Do you think a cat would ever call?

I'm waiting.

So are you.

JUDGE SCOTTOLINE
LISA

Lately, you're not allowed to be judgmental.

Or as people say, judgy.

And I get that.

I'm on board.

I used to be very judgy, and believe it or not, I wanted to be a critic when I grew up.

I'm not even kidding.

As soon as I got old enough to read movie and book reviews, I wanted to be the person who tells everybody what's good and what isn't.

Because back then, it used to be okay to have an opinion.

Mother Mary was the queen of opinions.

She had opinions about everything, all of them strongly held, but she didn't go on and on, expressing her opinion.

She didn't even use words.

She used a set of hand gestures, like Italian-American sign language.

Her favorite gesture was flicking her

fingers under her chin, which was the universal sign for disapproval, annoyance, or disrespect. It also doubled as the F word, only signed, in case you were deaf and/or polite.

The same gesture got the late Associate Justice Antonin Scalia of the Supreme Court in trouble, many years ago. A reporter for a Boston tabloid asked him a question he didn't like, and Justice Scalia flicked his fingers under his chin, just the way my mother always did. The reporter claimed the gesture was obscene, but Scalia denied it, claiming that it was merely "a gesture of indifference."

I can tell you right now, it was much more than indifference.

Italian-Americans don't do indifference.

We're emotional people, and we veer crazily back and forth between love and hate, which is just how we like it.

And implicit in that is judgment, which is exactly what I felt today, when I saw a newspaper article talking about women eating their placenta.

Yes, you read that right.

But please, tell me you didn't do that.

Evidently, it's the latest craze among celebrities, whereby women are saving their placenta and eating it raw, cooked, or having it freeze-dried into pills.

Can we judge?

The article I saw said that medical science was trying to get the word out that placenta eating had no health benefits whatsoever and could even be harmful.

But honestly, couldn't you have guessed that?

And does it matter?

Because no matter what the health benefits were, I wouldn't eat my own placenta.

And I wouldn't eat yours either.

Nothing personal.

But I never eat organ meat.

Especially not my own.

And I'm a vegetarian.

I became one when I read the article about people eating their placenta.

What do you serve with placenta?

Steamed broccoli?

Rice?

One celebrity had her placenta chopped into pieces and frozen, so she could put the pieces in a breakfast smoothie.

And how smooth can a smoothie be if it's full of placenta?

Either way, I'm judging.

Not a good idea.

In fact, a terrible idea.

And another terrible idea I read about was

some poor young woman who thought it would be a great idea to dye the white part of her eye purple, because she loves the color purple. And sadly, she ended up in a hospital and might go blind because she got an infection in her eye, from the needle that was used to inject the purple dye.

This is evidently called "body mod," or body modification, because she also has cut her tongue lengthwise, making it forked, in addition to an array of more normal tattoos and piercings.

Sorry, "normal" sounds judgy.

But when it's this far-out, let's judge.

In fact, let's have a judgy party.

Where is common sense?

What are we doing with our bodies?

Cooking our organs, dyeing our eyes?

Come over my house.

I'll teach you some useful Italian hand gestures.

And that will say it all.

The Great Makeup
Organization
FRANCESCA

My bathroom is covered in makeup.

Lipsticks and lip balms live on every ledge and sometimes end up in the dog's mouth. The closed toilet seat cover is a staging area for foundation and blushes. Brushes peek out of a coffee mug that barely fits on the counter. Eye-shadow compacts litter the sink's edge, daring to be knocked off and shatter on the floor.

In my defense, my bathroom is so small, three things out of place make it look like a disaster zone.

And I never have only three things out of place.

I don't let it stay like this. When someone is coming over, or when the chaos gets to me, I feverishly sweep all of my scattered items into various overstuffed gift-with-purchase cosmetics bags.

The cosmetics bags have a ranking system that only I know: The denim one is for the current, heavy-use rotation makeup items. I could probably throw out all but this one and not notice. The beat-up black bag is really meant to only hold brushes, but instead it's stuffed with former-favorite lipsticks, lesser-used eyeliners, and free samples.

The dog-hair-magnet Vera Bradley bag lives under my sink, I rarely open it and I don't remember what's in it, but sometimes I stuff something else into it when I'm in a fit of cleaning desperation.

All have dried-out, rancid mascaras mixed throughout.

They say you're supposed to throw out mascara every three months.

Do they think I'm made of money?

My mascara gets thrown out only when it smells like rotten eggs or gives me pink eye, whichever comes first.

Until then, I will rake those crusty bristles through my lashes like they owe me money.

Because they do. I don't even want to know the profit margin on a tube of Great Lash. And too often, I will buy a new mascara on impulse but still not throw the old one away, so it's a surprise which one gets opened each morning, the fresh or the stinky.

Which brings me to my recent epiphany. I

was on Sephora.com searching for the perfect bright berry lipstick, scouring reviews with an intensity that ought to be reserved for reading medical charts, when I was overcome with déjà vu.

Hadn't I already hunted down the perfect bright berry lipstick?

I went down to my bathroom and performed an archeological dig to find the Bite Beauty lipstick I bought last year. I twisted open the cap in triumph, only to be hit with the sour Play-Do scent of all-natural ingredients past their sell-by date.

And I only wore it twice. Twenty bucks down the drain because I didn't keep better track of my cosmetics.

I'd had enough. I was sick of having my stuff all over the place, wasting money losing things, wasting time looking for it, etc.

My bathroom has less than twenty-five square feet of floor space. The only storage is a medicine chest, which is already full, and three recessed wall shelves, seventeen inches wide and a mere three inches deep. If I was going to organize my makeup collection with this limited storage, I was going to need the help of the one store every messy person loves and fears:

The Container Store.

I love and hate The Container Store. It's a

cheap high of false promises. Take a hit, and all your messy-person problems will disappear.

Then the buzz wears off, and you're lost in the wilderness of a thousand boxes as empty as your soul.

If I thought The Container Store was overwhelming in person, I quickly learned that online, it's even worse. I scrolled through pages upon pages of, well, containers, and because they were only images against a white screen, I had no sense of size or scale without clicking to read the dimensions, which made finding what I needed painstaking and tedious. I had to search through no fewer than *two hundred and forty* "makeup organization" products before I found clear, stackable acrylic items that could fit on my tiny shelves.

I dusted off my high-school geometry skills to maximize my 153 square inches of space. I diagrammed my shelves on a legal pad, mapping out my options with different combinations of the miniature modular containers like Tetris pieces.

I should've drawn my calculations on the windows like in *A Beautiful Mind.* Sure, John Nash advanced the study of differential equations, but did he understand contouring?

When the containers arrived the next week, of course I'd messed up somehow and they didn't all fit, forcing me to improvise — but I was inspired. I could sense for the first time that organization was within my reach.

I purged my makeup stash. Everything got opened and tested to see if it deserved a spot in this new, glittering, acrylic-crystal utopia. I found the courage to throw away cosmetics I'd been holding on to since my college-theater-makeup-artist days. My waste bin became a mascara graveyard.

Maybelline they rest in peace.

It took a few hours, but I had done it — a place for everything and everything in its place. I took a photo to send to my mom, because she's known my makeup-strewn bathrooms since my middle-school years, when I would do a full face of makeup before bed to practice my techniques. (I still do this sometimes, by the way.) She had to see it now, looking so tidy and perfect, or she'd never believe me.

When I lowered my iPhone camera, I noticed I had two empty spots in my brand-new tiered lipstick organizer.

Hmph. I thought, *I could actually buy a couple new.*

Good thing I took that picture.

Because God knows how long it will stay this way.

Title: **The pillars of the earth**
Author: Follett, Ken
Item ID: U190302079784
Due: **10/24/2018**

Title: **The Secret, Book &
Scone Society [text
(large print)]**
Author: Adams, Ellery
Item ID: U190302426000
Due: **10/24/2018**

Title: **I see life through rose-
colored glasses [text
(large print)]**
Author: Scottoline, Lisa
Item ID: U190302426262
Due: **10/24/2018**

# of Items checked out in this transaction: 3

TRYHARD
LISA

Mother Mary knew the secret to great parenting.

Don't try too hard.

And I mean that in the best way.

The thing that both of my parents gave us in abundance was love.

That came naturally to them.

They didn't have to try very hard at all.

My brother Frank and I were adored, unconditionally.

They thought everything we did was great.

It was the only thing they agreed on, until they divorced.

Their love for us was all out of proportion with any reality. For example, I remember getting ready with my brother to go with my father to the World's Fair in New York City.

Yes, that would be in 1964.

Welcome to The History Channel, or in other words, my life.

I was born in 1955, so I was nine years old at the time.

Believe it or not, I just had to get a pencil and paper to do the math, including carrying-the-one, which shows my great affection for you.

I remember telling my mother that I was excited about seeing New York.

And I remember distinctly what she said to me, which was, "Honey, New York is excited to be seeing you."

Wow.

That's love.

Or maybe delusional behavior.

But either way, I grew up feeling pretty great about myself.

And not because I got good grades in school or for any other reason, except the fact that I breathed in and out.

My father was the same way.

I remember that after I had become an author he would come to my signings, and someone said to him, "You must be very proud of your daughter" and he said, "Lady, I was proud of her the day she came out of the egg."

I've told that story before, I tell it all the time, because I think I have the same attitude, and think it's one of the reasons that Francesca and I are so close.

I just adored her, the moment she came out of the egg.

I still do.

And I said all the dumb things to her that my mother said to me, like "don't study so much" and "it doesn't matter whether you get A's, just so you're happy" and "stop reading so much, it will ruin your eyes."

And paradoxically, Francesca turned out to be a wonderful student and accomplished great things, despite me telling her that she didn't need to bother.

And I can't say I caused that, or even that I planned it, only that when I think back to my childhood, I realize that there was absolutely no trying going on in my household, at all.

We just were.

And that applied to little things as well, like Halloween costumes.

Nowadays, Halloween costumes have been raised to an art form and there are parades in my town, where they give out a variety of prizes for the most original costume and such. All of the costumes are homemade, and I can see how hard the parents and kids tried to make a wonderful costume.

But we Scottolines never tried that hard.

For Halloweens when I was growing up, my mother went to Woolworth's and bought a costume in a box. It had a plastic mask that was stiff and attached to your face with a cheap piece of elastic that would undoubtedly break by the end of the evening.

Which was fine because the mask was too hot to wear anyway.

You could've welded in my Halloween mask.

I remember being Cleopatra five years in a row, and thinking back on it now, I realize I wore the same costume.

I mean the same *exact* costume, which my mother must have reboxed after Halloween and put away, only to present to me the next October.

"Cleopatra!" I would say with delight, each time.

Because for me, Halloween was when you got to be Cleopatra.

No one ever suggested you could actually change costumes, and I couldn't imagine why you would want to.

If you could be Cleopatra, why would you be anybody else?

I had diva tendencies even then.

Which Mother Mary evidently encouraged, being something of a diva herself, even though she was only four foot eleven inches.

Size really does not matter, people.

The costume was a sheath of turquoise polyester with pseudo-Egyptian hieroglyphics on the front, and the mask was authentically Cleopatran because it had triangle hair on either side of the face, a snake for a headband, and really bad eyeliner.

And I remember loving Halloween, with my father taking us from house to house, me swanning around in my Cleopatra dress and my brother in his pirate headscarf with a fake-silky blouse.

He was a pirate for five years in a row, too.

That was before we knew he was gay.

But he did look damn good in that blouse.

We'd carry paper bags to collect the candy and orange cartons to collect pennies for UNICEF, though we had no idea what that meant, only that it was a good thing to do and made a lot of noise when you shook the container.

All my memories of Halloween, like most of my childhood, are happy, filled with polyester, preservatives, and sugar.

We were happy because we loved each other and it showed.

My parents told us so, and hugged us, and kissed us.

When we fell and skinned a knee, it was a tragedy.

No injuries were ever walked off in the Scottoline household.

They were fussed over, worried about, and cured with food.

No failures or setbacks were ever shrugged off and anytime we were rejected by anybody or anything, fists were shaken.

"It's their loss," my father would always say.

And my mother would curse.

One time, in my lawyer days, she wanted to go to my law firm to yell at one of the partners for working me too hard.

I stopped her, saving the day.

For them.

Because an entire law firm was no match for my mother.

Now, that's love.

BAD DATE, GOOD STORY

FRANCESCA

"Okay, your turn: what's the worst date you've ever been on?"

I was at dinner with two friends of mine, my best friend from college and one from the city. We were already on our second round of rosé.

I shot a look to my bestie. "You know the one."

"Ohhh, with *Greg*!*" she recalled with a cackle. (*Names have been changed to protect the not-so-innocent.)

"Wait, do I know this story?" my other friend asked.

"It's too long, and she's heard it before," I said.

"Who cares? It's so good, I want to hear it again."

"Omigod, tell it."

My sophomore year of college, I started dating this guy, Greg. He was handsome,

341

chivalrous, and had wooed me with a dozen roses on our first date. I had only dated my high-school boyfriend before him, so I was swept off my feet.

Which is not to say I didn't have my doubts about Greg. We were obviously very different people. He was from Tampa and wore cowboy boots every day, except when he was working out for two hours a day in service of his hobby, natural bodybuilding. I thought he was sweet and quirky.

Not many dates in, he invited me to a Brooks and Dunn concert. He pitched this like it was a huge gift to me, but I'm not a Brooks and Dunn fan. I had to Google them. The only problem was the concert was in Connecticut, more than two hours away.

"We can stay overnight at my uncle's house. He's cool, you'll love him."

I hadn't yet spent the night with Greg, and now we were going to have our first sleepover at his uncle's. I wasn't in love with the idea, but I understood Greg was excited to share this band with me and introduce me to a family member, so I appreciated it.

The weekend of the concert, a snowstorm was rolling in. I secretly hoped we would bail, but Greg was determined. We drove all the way there, only to learn that the concert was canceled due to the snow. The roads had grown hazardous, so we found ourselves stranded at his uncle's house.

His uncle was a bachelor whose home, I quickly learned, was a house of midlife-crisis horrors. It was a McMansion he had all to himself, decorated in the generic way that made me think it might have been the display home for the development. Searching for something nice to say, I complimented a large vase of lilies, if only to get his eyes off me.

His uncle burst into laughter. "Fooled ya! They aren't real."

I touched the flowers and realized they were fabric.

"Think those look good, why don't you take a bite of that apple." He pointed to a fruit bowl on the kitchen island.

I touched it. "It's wax?"

He proceeded to show me with pride that the flowers, fruit, and — get this — the *eggs in the refrigerator* were all fake.

I can only imagine my shocked face because now they were both laughing. I smiled politely. "I understand the flowers, but why the eggs?"

"The ladies like to see it in the morning," his uncle said with a wink.

He could've spared me the wink. I got the

message the third time he called women "the ladies."

Since we were snowed out of the concert, Greg's uncle invited us to join him and his girlfriend at dinner.

Or, not girlfriend.

"Which number is this one?" Greg joked.

"The redhead." He implied he had quite the roster, which, to me, seemed impossible. When his date was delayed in the snow herself, his uncle quipped, "If she doesn't show, Greg, we can just share."

My skin crawled. I kept searching Greg for a knowing glance, a hand squeeze, any hint of validation that his uncle was being inappropriate, but I got nothing. I simultaneously hoped the woman would arrive as backup and that the weather would save her from Uncle Roofie.

Unfortunately for her, she made it, and we went to a late dinner. Neither Greg nor I were twenty-one, but his uncle ordered wine for the table, making sure I got a generous pour.

Before the appetizers even arrived, Greg knocked over my very full wineglass, splashing Cabernet all over the center of my cream-colored sweater dress.

"Nice one, Greg, but there are easier ways to get her dress off!" his uncle joked as I hurried to the bathroom.

A waitress brought me seltzer in the ladies' room, but there was no hope. I looked like Goldie Hawn in *Death Becomes Her.*

I rejoined the table. Even with three napkins on my chest and lap, I felt chilled in my damp clothes. But I tried to make the best of it. I could tell Greg was embarrassed, and I didn't want him to feel bad, my sole protector.

Back at his uncle's house, Greg suggested we use the hot tub on the deck. With the snow falling in the dark woods, it was very romantic, and I was thrilled to have broken free of our double date.

We were kissing in the hot tub, when suddenly the lights in the house went on.

I could see two people embracing and stumbling into the room off the deck. "Omigod, it's your uncle."

Greg chuckled. "I guess their date's going well!"

"I thought that was the guest room," I said. "How are we going to get back in?" The lights in the room went off again, with our clothes and shoes now locked inside.

"Oh, shi—"

We were forced to jump out of the hot water, scamper barefoot through the snow around the house to the front door, where, mercifully, Greg found a spare key so we did not freeze to death.

The whole afternoon and evening had been such a disaster, it had taken my mind off spending the night with Greg for the first time. I figured the night couldn't go any worse, right?

"Omigod, this is the best part. We need more wine." My best friend peered around for the waiter.

"What happened?"

"Okay, okay, so listen." I continued:

So, we're in bed, and Greg compliments my body. I've never taken a compliment that well, especially now that it's coming from someone who literally spends hours in the gym perfecting his physique, so I don't remember what exactly I said, but I dismissed it in the way women do.

He recoils and gives me this incredulous look. "You *seriously* don't think you have a great body?"

I giggle nervously. "I dunno . . ."

He goes, "That's it!" and springs out of bed. He whips off the comforter and the top sheet clear off the bed, like a magician tearing away a tablecloth.

I am completely exposed. "What are you doing?"

But he's not finished. He grabs me by the wrists and pulls me out of the bed. He drags me to the bathroom, and I try to pull away, but his grip is so tight it twists the skin on my wrists.

"Greg, stop! I don't like this, you're freaking me *out*!"

He stops in the bathroom and flips on all the bright overhead lights, still not letting me go. He's holding my wrists to his chest in a way that could almost be romantic if I weren't fully restrained, and he shushes me. "Shh, shh, listen to me."

Then, without warning, he yanks my arms high above my head and spins me around to face the full-length mirrors on the wall. I see myself stretched out, completely naked, looking absolutely terrified.

He says, "Look at yourself," before lowering his face to the nape of my neck, getting so close I can feel his breath, and he whispers, *"You're perfect."*

"Stop it!" my friend cut in. "That's the creepiest thing I've ever heard."

"Oh, believe me, for a minute there, I legitimately thought he might kill me. Like, *you're perfect . . . for me to wear your skin.*"

■ ■ ■ ■

Having found my fight-or-flight adrenaline strength, I break free and shove him off. He tries to play it off innocently.

"What? I just wanted you to see how beautiful you are."

I really think in his brain, this was a cute rom-com moment and not *Amityville Horror.*

Of course, I did not sleep. I lay awake all night, trying to process the whole thing. By the morning, I was exhausted, pissed off, and desperate to get out of there. Greg is completely oblivious, suggesting we play a board game while his uncle and his date take their time waking up. I'm having none of it. I sit next to my packed suitcase in the living room and wait.

Finally, Greg's uncle and his date wake up. His uncle swaggers into the kitchen all pleased with himself, his date pads in wearing his clothes as PJs.

"How about I make some breakfast for all of us?" she offers, opening the fridge. "How do you like your eggs?"

"They're fake," I blurt out. "They're *fake eggs*! See?" I push past her to the refrigerator door, take out a wooden egg, and wrap it against the kitchen counter.

I actually felt like I got through to her, sister to sister. She looks at Greg's uncle. "Really? Why would you —"

But I've come undone. "It's all fake! The fruit, the flowers, everything in here!" I couldn't stop myself. I was like Mr. Rochester's first wife, free from the attic. They would either heed my warning or cast me out, I didn't care, either was better than being trapped in that house.

Sure enough, after my meltdown, Greg got me right out of there. He was mad at me for busting his uncle and being rude in general, but I didn't care.

"Thank *God* you got free," said my friend.

My best friend nodded. "It actually gets crazier hearing it again. I blocked out parts."

I raised my glass. "To friends and freedom."

We all toasted: "To friends and freedom!"

And the good stories along the way.

Move Over, Laika

LISA

There is yet another study by academics about sleeping with dogs.

That doesn't apply to me.

The new study by the Mayo Clinic says that people who sleep with one dog in their bedroom, but not on their bed, will sleep better.

I bet that's true.

But it bears no relationship to my life.

Okay, it's the Mayo Clinic, so they must know what they're talking about.

And I'll take them at their word.

I bet if I had just one dog, and somehow managed to keep it off the bed, that I would sleep better.

There are a lot of things like that, which may be true in an alternative universe.

If I were younger, I could win an Olympic gold medal.

If I were better-looking, I could become a supermodel.

And if I were smarter, I would know how to train my dogs to stay off of the bed.

But I'm not any of the above.

And neither are my dogs.

First, I have five dogs, not just one.

I look back fondly on the days when I had an only dog.

It was so much easier.

I could give her treats and not worry about their causing fights.

I could buy her toys and not worry about them being stolen by the other dogs.

I could give her attention and not worry about the other dogs being jealous.

But those days lasted about thirty seconds before the second dog came along, then the third, fourth, fifth, and maybe I need to start using birth control.

However I got here, here I am, with my little pack of five crazies.

And I love it, except at night.

Because five of us sleep on the bed together, and I guarantee you, anybody who sleeps with four dogs is not getting as good a night's sleep as somebody who doesn't.

You feel me, Mayo Clinic?

I'm not complaining, because if I wanted to, I suppose I could lock them out of the bedroom and put up with their scratching on the door all night.

But I love sleeping with them, and it's fun.
It isn't restful, however.

Anybody who has little dogs knows that they want to sleep near your head, not at the foot of the bed, like in catalogs and TV commercials.

So that means I'm sharing the pillow most nights with one or two dogs, and more specifically, their butts.

Here is the thing about sleeping dogs:

They're always upside down.

Invariably if you're sleeping with the dog, you will start out with its head toward the headboard, just like yours. But sometime during the night, all the dogs will shift on their rotational axis, obeying magnetic fields in the universe, which they obey more readily than you.

And you will wake up in the morning looking at your dog's butt.

"Wake up and smell the coffee" doesn't apply to dog owners.

Because that's not what I smell most mornings.

Or during the night.

I'm not sure the Mayo Clinic has addressed this question.

And Ruby The Crazy Incontinent Corgi raises a special problem, in terms of bedtime.

Yes, we're going there.

As I have mentioned, she has a disorder that has left her paralyzed, so that she can't use any of her limbs anymore, not even her cart. But she's not in any pain, and she's still her happy, healthy, and bossy self from the neck up, so I keep her in a diaper and set her on a wee-wee pad, like her own personal launchpad.

We think positive in the Scottoline household.

You're not paralyzed, you're just pretakeoff.

T minus 1,937,466,365 and counting.

I mean, dogs have flown in space.

Why not Astronaut Ruby?

But to return to my point, Ruby's the only dog who sleeps at the foot of the bed, and so far, so good.

Until she started moving around during the night, and since she's less than coordinated, she would actually roll off the bed.

Does a bedroom get any sexier?

Four farting dogs and a rolling astronaut in a diaper.

Hubba hubba.

Ruby fell twice, so I had to figure what to do. I decided the safest thing was to put her and her launchpad next to the bed, but on the floor. This is not going so well, which is the current reason I'm losing sleep.

Because she wants to be back on the bed.

And she wants to boss the other dogs around.

And she wants her legs to work again.

So sometimes during the night, she gets unhappy and whimpers, which wakes me up.

I could make her sleep in the kitchen, so I couldn't hear her whimper, but I have a heart.

Her life sucks enough without her being exiled from our sleepless, gassy family den.

So my next move is to figure out how to make a wall on the foot of the bed, so she can't roll off.

I'm going to ask the Mayo Clinic what to do.

Because they're so damn smart.

BASIC AND PROUD OF IT
FRANCESCA

In the summer I drink rosé.

In the fall I drink Pumpkin Spice Lattes.

In the winter I wear Uggs.

All year long, I wear black yoga pants to do everything but yoga.

I watch every show on Bravo.

I'm basic and proud of it.

I don't remember exactly when I became aware of what "basic" meant as it refers to women. Probably whatever belated point new slang passes through black culture, then gay culture, then teen culture, before coming to rest among millennial white women.

Basic means mainstream, lame, unoriginal. It is used most frequently in reference to women, often with an expletive:

Basic bitch.

I can see how, among a marginalized group, "basic" as a putdown expresses an empowering reversal of power in an unjust social hierarchy.

If society doesn't accept you the way you are, screw them, they're just basic.

I love it used that way!

But as often happens, something got lost in translation when the term was appropriated by a wider audience. Now it seems the term "basic" has become a sexist dig used to undermine women and mock those things that women enjoy.

Specifically, those things we enjoy without men's agreement or approval.

They don't like how we look in Uggs.

They don't prefer sweet, flavored coffee.

They don't drink pink wine.

(Or they do, and they have to pretend like they don't, because that's *girl stuff.*)

I think they're missing out. Women have excellent taste.

There's an irony, of course, in using the notion of generic "basicness" of women against them, when women are otherwise pilloried for not fitting into the narrow parameters society lays down for us.

Everything about women is more unique than society would like us to be. We're too many different shapes and sizes, our hair too many different textures, our opinions too loud and too varied, our orgasms too complicated.

Why should we apologize for our preferences? If many women, in all our glorious variations, agree that something is pretty great, maybe it is.

Uggs are comfortable. I don't care if they're ugly. Neither do Uggs, they tell you so right in the name.

Do you know how many women's fashion items privilege comfort over appearance? One: Uggs.

That's hardly basic; it's downright subversive.

Same with yoga pants. Do you know how much a woman can get done in a day? On any given Saturday, she needs to run across town, and bend to pick up the kids, and stretch to reach the top shelf at the grocery, and sit working on the computer.

They expect us to do all that in skinny jeans?

Believe me, namaste or not, a woman's life warrants a performance material.

Perhaps the most absurd assumption about the "basic bitch" is a beverage choice or a love of elastic tells you everything there is to know about her.

The idea that the superficial explains the interior is straight out of the sexist playbook, and women should reject it, not use it against each other.

The patriarchy is the *original* basic bitch.

Case in point: I was recently on the dating app Bumble, and I saw a guy whose bio read, "My type: NOT a girl wearing yoga pants and Uggs with a PSL attached to her hand."

Mind you, this man's profile also said he worked in finance, went to Cornell, and enjoyed hiking, travel, and "good food."

A true original!

I swiped right only to message him: "Finance bros in glass office buildings shouldn't throw stones."

He did not reply.

Sadly, I didn't have to wonder about the strategy of putting down the basic girl in his dating profile. Dating apps allow wannabe pickup artists to *neg* with a wide net, in other words, use the ploy that denigrating a swath of women will attract one via our competitive spirit and our desire to prove ourselves worthy of his approval.

Pick me, I'm not like other women, I'm different and better.

Too often, it works.

When sexism in our society communicates to women, you're interchangeable, you're replaceable, you're disposable, *you're basic,* we're inclined to defend ourselves by saying, "Not me."

But a better answer to that nonsense is, *"Not us."*

Otherwise, we're playing by the rules they give us, even as we know the game is rigged. When women adopt the tactics men use to diminish us, we all lose.

I once asked an old boyfriend to stop using the word "slut" because it offended me. His defense was that it shouldn't because the word didn't apply to me, I was classy and deserving of respect, unlike *some women.*

This is some basic bullshit.

Sisters, beware. Beware the trap of elevating yourself by trampling on other women. First, it's wrong. And second, it doesn't work. What undermines one of us undermines all.

The only solution is sisterhood.

And that doesn't mean sameness. Sisterhood means less judgment of each other, less negative comparison. It means greater acceptance, compassion, and expression of all our different views.

And some shared ones.

Pass the rosé.

Technology Hag
LISA

I'm not old, but I'm getting older.

I know this because of technology.

Meanwhile, where do I even begin with the story?

Let's start with the time a few months ago, when I trip over a dog gate, go flying, and can't walk.

I've been hobbling around since then.

Seriously, I'm bent over like the old witch in *Snow White.* Plus I have stringy gray hair and a big nose.

All I need is the carbuncle.

Oh, wait.

Never mind.

Check.

But not the point herein.

I hobble around for about three weeks, barely able to straighten up, much less sit or drive, and so I finally get my butt to an orthopedist, who takes an MRI and tells me that I have a labral tear in my hip.

At first I thought I heard him wrong.

I didn't think my labral was in my hip.

I got it mixed up with another body part, which should give you an idea of how good I was at sex.

Kind of not very.

But honestly, who cares anyway?

I'm great at writing!

Anyway, it turns out that a labral tear is a tear in the ligament that's somewhere in your hip joint, and when I leave the doctor's office, he gives me a DVD of my MRI.

Like a party favor for the middle-aged.

I take it home, and the first thing I want to do is look at my MRI.

Which is when I realized that I don't have a DVD player in any of my computers.

What?

I don't even know when that happened.

I seem to remember that I got new computers a year or so ago, because I like to have a nice big screen. And I don't mind spending the money, because all I do all day is stare at a computer, and the least I can do is have a nice one. But I never really noticed that they didn't have a slot for a DVD player.

So I went over to my big TV, figuring that I could watch my MRI on TV, like a medical reality show, maybe one called, *Your*

Labral Isn't What You Think It Is.

I managed to locate my DVD player underneath the TV, but it needed to be hooked up, since I am addicted to Netflix and haven't watched a real DVD in a long time. It took me a full hour of struggling to hook it up, and even then, I couldn't get it to work.

Which is when it struck me.

I am so ancient that I have lived through several stages of technology, like the Jurassic and Pleistocene era of dinosaurs.

I remember when there were VHS tapes because I still have them.

I remember when there were camcorders because I filmed Francesca when she was a baby, plus static scenes of my feet, with me saying, "Is this thing on or off?"

Now I have lived through DVDs, which sucks, because I have an entire set of operas on DVD that I was saving to watch in my retirement, and by the time I retire, operas will be transported telepathically into your brain.

Plus I paid to have those camcorder tapes of Francesca transferred onto DVDs, and now there's no such thing as DVD players.

So you're getting a fairly complete picture of what life is like as me, which I'm hoping is like life as you too.

Who here remembers actual records?

I do.

Who remembers little 45s?

I do.

Who remembers cassette tapes?

I do.

How about trying to rewind them and having them unspool out of the slot like brown tinsel?

I know. Me too.

So there you have it. Many of us live a life measured in obsolete technological stages.

It's enough to make your hip hurt.

MULTIPLES

LISA

Yes, I have multiples.

Not orgasms.

Pets.

Which honestly, is almost as much fun.

At least as far as I can remember.

Maybe having a bad memory is merciful.

I don't really want to remember how great sex was, now that I'm not having any.

The same goes for banana splits, which I used to love.

Haven't had one of those in ages.

They weren't that good, were they?

Anyway, to stay on point, as I have mentioned, I have five dogs, but what always amazes me is how remarkably different their personalities are, each in its own way. If you have even a single pet, dog, cat, parrot, or even lizard, you know exactly what I'm talking about.

Okay, I'm tempted to say maybe not lizards, but isn't that the whole point?

When you don't really know about something, you do tend to dismiss its entire category. I think it happens with people, but it also happens with animals, too. For a long time we didn't understand how intelligent and sentient animals like cows and pigs were, but now it's well known that pigs are as smart as most dogs.

As soon as I learned that, I stopped eating pork.

And I took my dogs to obedience school.

Which didn't take.

Only one of the dogs, namely Boone, was interested in pleasing me, but he got so excited during the class he couldn't sit still. It turned out to be a problem, since he was trying to learn the command, "Go to your place." It meant that he had to go sit on a platform, but he got so excited every time he sat on the platform that he fell off twice.

You're probably wondering what kind of wacky obedience class this was, and I will tell you, it was my mistake.

I knew that the dogs had been behaving badly, but I didn't do anything about it until one day I just got fed up and I decided that they were going to school. The only problem was that all the basic obedience classes were full, and the only class that had any openings was Circus Tricks.

Did that stop me?

Of course not.

I was desperate for them to learn something, and they're five years old, so it's not as if they can get into a puppy class. And I refused to believe that you can't teach an old dog new tricks, because God knows I've learned a few.

So I took the two worst-behaved dogs, brothers Boone and Kit, to the Circus Tricks class on separate nights, and you can imagine how that went.

A three-ring circus.

Kit is timid, so I thought the socialization would help him, but the tricks gave him pause.

Or paws.

For example, one of the tricks was to jump in a suitcase and close the lid.

It sounds dumb when you say it, but it really is a supercute trick, and his brother Boone loved doing it. Even today, if I'm packing to go on book tour and I leave my suitcase on the floor, he'll jump right in and pull the lid over his head with his mouth.

Good boy!

You haven't lived until you've seen a dog pack himself.

But Kit had the opposite reaction. He was completely intimidated by the suitcase trick, and I get that.

Who wants to entomb themselves for fun?

So I couldn't get Kit to go anywhere near the suitcase in class, and now whenever I pack for book tour, he runs under the bed in fear.

So you see, the class really helped.

I stuck it out until the bitter end, but all three of us flunked.

And the dogs remain disobedient, if adorable.

The most adorably disobedient is Peach, who is Boone and Kit's mother.

She's my favorite, but I feel guilty even saying that. Still, she's my cuddle monster and we love each other, a fact she completely forgets every night when I let the dogs in the backyard to go to the bathroom and have to get them back in. Every dog except Peach comes in right away, not because I call them, but because they're tired.

My dogs can't wait to go to bed.

If I'm working late in my office downstairs, Boone and Little Tony will go to the landing on the stairs and fall asleep there to give me guilt.

Kit will head upstairs to bed and start watching Kimmel.

Only Peach will stay in the backyard, bark-

Cavaliers: You can't have just one!

ing and barking at God knows what. I can call her for half an hour but she won't come. Invariably, I have to get the flashlight, go out, and find her.

You would think she'd be the best behaved because she's the mother.

But now that I think about it, maybe that's why she's the least well behaved.

It's tiring to keep those kids in line all day.

She just wants to have a little fun and bark at the moon.

Inside every mother is a party animal.

Party on.

RequiAIM

FRANCESCA

Ladies and gentlemen, we are gathered here today to mourn the passing of an old friend, AOL Instant Messenger.

This December, after twenty years of service, the away message will be up for good.

AIM is being laid to rest.

AIM was the first love that paved the way for today's texting obsession. It was the originator of text-shortening slang, *lol, jk, omg.* It saved us from the creepy free-for-alls that were AOL chat rooms. For me, it was the site of all my adolescent dramas, great and small.

Do you remember your screen name?

Mine was Geoslab.

I got the name from a random font I liked. I chose it because it was gender-neutral (I had learned my lesson of the dangers of being openly female in AOL chat rooms), and because I thought it sounded like something from *The Matrix.*

When any friend asked what the name meant, I refused to tell them — a very cool move at the time.

It was my first and last time being mysterious.

It was not my first or last time being a little bit dumb.

AIM is where I learned to touch type. We had typing class in middle school, but I didn't appreciate the power of asdfjkl; until I needed to reply to my crush ASAP.

Mavis Beacon couldn't motivate me like Andrew from Social Studies.

AIM is where I learned to flirt. The chime of a new IM, instant message, could probably still make my heart skip a beat.

In person, I was a studious, thirteen-year-old girl who acted superior to the boys because I was pretty much terrified of them. The boys at that age rarely looked up through their bangs.

But it's easier to be brave behind a screen. On AIM, nerds could have Nora Ephron-worthy banter.

And if I couldn't think of something witty to say, I could always just say, *brb, g2g,* my mom needed the phone line.

My best guy friend and I talked endlessly on AIM. At school, we were completely platonic, but online, we were Harry and Sally.

It let us toe the romantic waters with each other — and with anyone! — for the first time. It took months of circling the idea on our online chats before we went on an actual date. The date was horribly awkward, as any outing that begins with being dropped off by your parents is doomed to be. But we recovered and tried again; our suave, AIM alter egos were able to smooth things out in the following days.

Most importantly, our conversations over AIM made me feel like he was attracted to my mind, not just my new bra size.

I feel terrible for the young girls these days who get pressured into texting or posting a picture to feel sexy. AIM let a teen girl *talk* sexy, which does a whole different thing for a young adult's self-esteem.

So much so, that when I had my heart broken over AIM, I was able to stand up for myself.

Like the time I was chatting with my senior, bad-boy crush. He was a moody wrestler that I tutored in French. I had loved him from afar for years. Right before he graduated, just in time for our love to feel impossible, we struck up an unlikely friendship. I didn't want to get ahead of myself, but it almost seemed like he liked me.

Like-liked me.

So when his screen name popped up in an AIM chat window, I knocked over the dog to get to the computer chair.

(A nostalgic pause for the days of one family desktop computer and designated "computer chair.")

So we got to IM'ing, and he asked me why I don't have a boyfriend.

Hoping it would prompt him to ask me out, I coyly answered, "I dunno, you tell me."

His reply was swift: "It's your nose. It's too big, and it doesn't have an angle at the end."

I felt the blood drain out of me. My number one insecurity, albeit one I rarely gave voice to, was my Italian schnoz. It was the physical flaw I zeroed in on in every photo but always hoped no one else noticed as much as I did. And here he said it, right to my face.

Well, to my computer screen.

And that was my saving grace — that AIM allowed me to have that moment of stunning, painful humiliation in the privacy of my own home. I paused, collected myself, and reclaimed my power.

"I'm well aware I don't have a little Britney Spears ski-jump nose. The boys in our school should be so lucky."

He tried to save it. "That's what I meant. You know, and you don't care, and *that's* what makes you sexy."

Nice try, pal. It was probably the first time anyone had explicitly called me sexy, much less someone I had crushed on forever, but the harsh light of the AOL window showed me the truth: he was just another fumbling teenage boy, and I didn't need to settle for a backhanded compliment.

He even went on to ask me out again and again (always online) and I told him no, he had hurt my feelings, and I wasn't interested.

In person, I could barely summon the confidence to correct his pronunciation of *quelle heure,* but on AIM I knew my worth.

There's a lot of talk about how technology has made teenage angst harder, and today that's undoubtedly true. I'm very grateful I didn't have to have my falling-out with the popular girls in fifth grade play out on Facebook or my pimples displayed on Instagram.

But millennials my age were in the sweet spot of tech-assisted growing pains. We weren't humiliated at the school dance like

Molly Ringwald, nor were we smeared in the virtual public square of social media.

Instead of being like a scary online girls' bathroom, AIM was like a good friend. It could get you out of a tough conversation with a simple signoff, and it had your back with a passive-aggressive away message.

Alanis Morissette lyrics, anyone?

In an ironic twist, good old AIM, my main tool of procrastination during high school, was instrumental in getting me accepted to college.

One of the essays I submitted was a real AIM dialogue between a boy and me, complete with our screen names in red and blue, and edited with my commentary.

In retrospect, it was the first time I spun a story of heartbreak for laughs, long before I ever imagined I could make a living doing so.

My one-act AIM play centered around the comical demise of my barely there relationship with that guy friend I mentioned before, my Harry. We had just started dating when he messaged me that he had a dilemma weighing on him that he wanted to discuss with me, because I'm "so easy to talk to."

He went on to explain that he liked me a lot, but he had just kissed an older girl and he thought he might like her too, and he just didn't know how to choose between us.

¯_(ツ)_/¯

I replied, "The way I see it, you have two choices. You can date her, or you can be single."

That's AIM confidence for you.

Because perhaps AIM's greatest lesson was that words have power.

Even if the words you use are stronger than you may feel in the moment, writing them out can bolster your spirit.

Words can *give* you power.

So thank you, AOL Instant Messenger, for your innocence and your excitement, your gentleness and your strength.

Until we meet again, *ily, ttyl.*

ADULTS ONLY
LISA

Lately, everyone's talking about adulting.

No, not adultery.

Nobody even knows that word anymore.

Adulting is a made-up word that means trying to be an adult and doing the daily things that adults have to do, like paying bills, putting out the recycling, and establishing a savings account.

Everyone online is talking and blogging about adulting, so much so that there's even a backlash against it, with people claiming it's sexist, boring, or overplayed.

That's where I come in.

At the end.

I always get wind of something when everyone else is sick of it.

Just like I always hit the store and find out the sale was last week.

But as for adulting, I'm a fan.

I'm even a fan of the word.

Usually I don't like trendy, made-up

words, but this one makes sense, and honestly, I've thought for a long time that adulthood should come with a basic book of instructions, so you know the myriad of things that are expected of you, from the macro level like Be Kind To People And Animals, down to the micro level like You Can Wash Your Hair With Dishwashing Liquid if You Run Out of Shampoo, and Vice Versa.

See, did you know that?

Well, it's true.

Take it from me.

Don't ask how I know.

To stay on point, maybe that's what happens as we get older. We accumulate all kinds of little tips for living, which not only help you do the right thing but also make your life easier.

For example, Tell The Truth is always the right thing.

But you know what will make your life easier?

You Can Pick Your Teeth With An Envelope If You Don't Have A Toothpick.

See?

That's a quality life tip, right there.

Let's call it adulting, so we feel trendy.

I read online that there was a library giving classes in adulting, and I applaud that.

It's just another thing to love about libraries, though between us, I feel like I could teach an adulting class, with tips like:

Clean The Lint Trap On The Dryer Or Something Bad Will Happen.

Change The Oil Filter On Your Car Or Something Bad Will Happen.

Don't Be Weird About Going To The Doctor Or Something Bad Will Happen.

We can all agree on those adulting tips. And then there are ones that only I know:

Drink Half & Half When You Run Out Of Milk Because It Tastes Like Milk, Only Better.

Don't Buy Foundation Because It Wears Off After Two Hours And If It Doesn't, It Was Too Thick In The First Place.

Don't Cut Your Hair When You Think You Need To Because That's When It's Starting To Look Good.

Buy Cheap Bras Because They're Always More Comfy Than Expensive Ones.

And, Buy Back-ups Of Everything, Especially Toilet Paper.

Agree or disagree?

But even though I have learned a few things, it doesn't necessarily mean that I'm supersuccessful as an adult.

In fact, I screwed up as an adult just today.

What happened was that yesterday afternoon, I was standing outside with the dogs and I felt a gnat around my face. I tried to wave it away, but by mistake, I batted it into my eye.

So right there, not quality adulting.

In fact, that's an epic fail, as the kids would say.

Of course, they said epic fail three years ago.

I just now got wind of it.

Which would probably be the definition of an epic fail.

But anyway, the gnat was in my eye, so I washed my eye and thought I'd gotten it out. It bothered me the rest of the day, but I figured it was irritated and forgot about it. I went to sleep, woke up the next morning, and looked in the mirror.

And what did I see?

Well, nothing, out of one eye.

It was all black.

Because there was a dead gnat on my cornea.

Yes, I slept all night with a bug in my eye.

It must have drowned in my eye juice.

But I slept great.

Maybe it was a sleeping bug?

Anyway, I'm not proud of this.

No matter how you slice it, it's not quality adulting.

I'm pretty sure that if I taught a course in adulting, the first lesson would have to be:

Don't Sleep With Bugs In Your Eyes.

So I'm not always perfect.

But above all, It's Okay Not To Be Perfect.

PROPORTION CONTROL

LISA

I just finished a draft of my next novel, and I typed The End.

As in the end of the book.

And of eating.

It's always the same.

It takes me six months to write a novel, and during that time, I sit on my butt 24/7 and eat carbohydrates, in the belief that they will help fuel my creativity.

Well, anything is possible.

And they could have a placebo effect.

Because I write better under the influence of carbs.

Leave the booze to Hemingway.

He famously said, "Write drunk, edit sober."

But I say, "Do both, with pretzels."

And while I work and eat, I imagine that I'm stoking some literary furnace, shoveling carbs into my mouth in the way they shoveled coal into locomotives or machinery or whatever they shoveled coal into, way back when.

It's not a pretty visual, but it gets the job done.

Carbs fuel my Industrial Revolution.

I get very industrious.

Also, carbs taste good.

And something about the crunching enhances productivity, as if your teeth are the gears in your own personal machine.

My go-to carb is popcorn, which I microwave myself on those rare occasions I feel like cooking.

You probably didn't imagine there was anything lazier than microwaving your meal, but there is, and it's me.

Most of the time, I buy big bags of already-popped popcorn, in Family Size.

Meanwhile, I'm one person.

But that doesn't stop me.

I count as a family.

In fact, I'm a growing family.

My butt and my waistline are growing.

But still, popcorn is one of the carbs you feel less guilty about on the carb spectrum.

I feel guiltier about my second go-to carb, which is Stacy's Pita Chips.

Don't even get me started.

I will simply set the bag beside the computer, write, and chip away at the chips.

Before I know it, the bag will be gone. In fact, sometimes I try to "eat them all gone," just like little kids say, because it's the only way I will ever stop.

It's not easy to write a novel, and there are some hard parts that will require next-level carbohydrates.

It's like you're fighting the battle, and popcorn and pita chips are the Army and Navy.

But sometimes you need to call in Special Forces.

Of course, we're talking potato chips.

Potato chips are the SEALs of carbohydrates.

Now listen, I know what you're thinking.

No woman who's trying to lose weight has any right being around an open bag of potato chips.

But what can I tell you?

Everything about potato chips is awesome. The salt, the crunch, and the grease on your fingers that you will suck off because you live alone.

You get the idea.

My main problem is portion control.

And if you gobble down carbs for six months, and the only exercise you get is walking to the microwave or driving to the supermarket, you're going to gain ten pounds.

Which is where I am.

So I started exercising like mad, walking the dogs until they beg for mercy, and I realize that I have to do something about portion control.

And I find myself in the store, ransacking the snack aisle for hundred-calorie bags of carbohydrates.

Yes, that's where we are.

I tell myself, it doesn't matter what the carb is, if there's only a hundred calories of it, I'll be fine.

Right?

Wrong.

Because the next step in the writing process is that I send the manuscript to my terrific editor, and she makes a lot of wonderful suggestions to the novel, which send me back to the drawing board for three more weeks.

And what's the first thing I do?

Fortify myself.

Stoke my creativity.

Start shoveling.

Hundred-calorie bags.

You know the commercial that says, "I bet you can't eat just one?"

I think they were talking about bags.

Because this bag can't eat just one bag.

I understand the thinking behind the hundred-calorie bags.

To show people like me what a hundred calories of pita chips looks like.

Now, that's an eye-opener.

It's about four chips and crumbs.

In other words, an appetizer.

But if you're the kind of person who has to buy hundred-calorie bags in order to control your portions, you're probably not the kind of person who's going to stop at just one bag.

I wish I could say I was.

But I'm not.

The hundred-calorie bags may slow me down, but they don't stop me.

I've eaten three at a stretch.

But you know what?

I'm fine with that.

Hard work is what made this country great.

If I have to eat my way to success, I will.

The End.

Handbag Time Machine
FRANCESCA

I was going through a closet at my mom's house when I spotted an old handbag I felt worthy of rescuing and bringing back to New York. Upon opening it, I found a folded piece of yellow paper inside. It had a list of questions written on it in my handwriting, that I didn't remember writing:

"In whose house was he raised? Yours or Barbara's?"

"How much does he eat, how often?"

"Introducing to other dogs?"

I pulled out the next items: two tickets to Dressage at Devon 2008.

Suddenly, my heart swelled at the memory.

I was transported to September 2008, when I first met Pip as a puppy. I had written these questions down because I was so nervous and excited, I was afraid I would forget to ask them.

Pip was called "Nino" back then, full

name Holyoke's Pinot Nino Grigio. He'd been carefully and responsibly bred to be a show dog, but he was available for adoption because of the unfortunate fact that he had only one descended testicle.

Unfortunate for the American Kennel Club — extremely fortunate for me.

I was fresh out of college, and I remember I intentionally wore my Harvard T-shirt and pearl earrings — a twenty-two-year-old's idea of a confidence-inspiring outfit — because I wanted to be seen as a qualified and trustworthy potential adopter. I rang the breeder's doorbell and heard a chorus of barking within. She opened the door holding a cherub in the form of a dog — a puppy so plump, fluffy, and perfect, I forced myself not to look directly at it.

That can't be him, I warned myself. *He's too tiny and cute, she would never part with that one, don't even hope.*

But it was my Pip. My little baby. My best friend I hadn't met yet.

I don't remember whether or not I bothered asking those questions. I had every answer I needed watching this precious puppy chase after a fallen leaf, tumble in the grass, and present his petal-pink belly for tummy rubs.

As in love as I was that first day, I had no

idea the joy Pip would bring me for the next ten years and hopefully more. I can't imagine life without him.

The sweet nostalgia made me wonder what I'd find inside my other old purses. I've always thought time capsules seemed like the coolest idea, but I'd never gone to the trouble of burying one. Now I wondered how many I had waiting for me in my closet back home.

The first one I dug out was a quilted brown bag I hadn't carried in years. Inside, I found a hotel room keycard, the business card for the Seventh Avenue New York Sports Club, and a Band-Aid.

The Band-Aid made it click — my first apartment-hunting trip to New York City, a marathon weekend of walking crosstown and up staircases — and the souvenir blisters.

Because I was young, dumb, and fun, I brought my new puppy with me on the apartment visits although I mostly ended up carrying him. Pip was only four months old, still acclimating to the leash, and, as a country puppy, wholly unprepared for the urban bouquet of smells. When I tried to walk him, he would take a few steps, then plop down onto the sidewalk in awe.

I remember wishing I could do the same.

Ultimately, I took that apartment near that Seventh Avenue New York Sports Club although I didn't make enough money to join. No matter. I got my exercise from taking the stairs to my sixth-floor apartment.

Next, I unearthed a canvas, zippered bag I hardly recognized. Inside, it held a worksheet on verb conjugations, tickets to two *musei,* and Italian international stamps — summer 2006, my study abroad in Abruzzo, Italy. I could almost feel the golden sunlight and taste the briny *linguine alle vongole* that I ate every day, *al fresco,* overlooking the Adriatic Sea.

By the end of that summer I was fluent, as proven in a real-life final exam of winning an argument with a hotheaded Roman hotel clerk, but more important than any language skills I gained, that was the summer when I solidified my friendship with the woman who would become my best friend from college to this day. Ten weeks together, fumbling through a foreign country, sleeping in a tiny motel room with no air-conditioning, and we didn't have a single fight — that doesn't make a friend, that makes a sister.

That trip was where we learned our personalities were perfectly complementary. I carried both of our passports in this handbag because she's forgetful and prone to losing things, while I compulsively check and double-check that I have everything. Meanwhile, she brought a little whimsy to our adventures. Like on a day trip to Venice, while the other girls on our program spent the evening in an Internet café talking to their boyfriends, my friend had the idea that we should change into our best dresses and go to Harry's Bar like old movie stars and drink Bellinis.

Or Bellini. They were so expensive, we had only enough Euros for one drink each.

But we were so happy and excited to be there, the waitstaff got a kick out of us, and they proceeded to bring us another round of Bellinis and a sampling of every dessert they made, *offerto dalla casa,* on the house.

I remember two English tourists seated nearby accused us of writing our phone numbers on the bill. They were surprised we were Americans.

"You giggle like British girls," one said, making us laugh harder.

(And lest you feel too bad for *our* boyfriends, I'll tell you I wrote to my college sweetheart every single day, sending old-fashioned love letters to the Air Force base where he was having field training — hence, the international stamps.)

Not every memory in these handbags has been so clear. In a tote bag with a broken strap, I found a printed card from J.Crew.com that read:

"HAPPY BIRTHDAY, STUD! Unwrap this, then I'll unwrap you;) I love you! Xoxo, F."

I forgot what a clever girlfriend I can be! Although I confess, I also forgot the gift and the stud recipient.

But I've only said *I love you* to three men in my life, and two of them called me by my old nickname, Kiki, so by process of elimination, I figured it out.

And he still wears that shirt I got him.

There was something especially sweet about finding these small mementos: the serendipity, the puzzle of them, the way the memories sneaked up on me. It's ironic that the most photographed generation has so few physical reminders like these. Now every memory is captured on a smartphone, the image digital and intangible, likely to be forgotten in the Cloud. Forgotten or lost — my laptop crashed in 2010, and I lost all the photos I had taken that summer in Italy. You can't stumble across an old digital image by accident unless you count those Facebook Memories that seem to only show me pictures of my exes, but there's little mystery or charm in an algorithm. I'd nearly forgotten the pleasure of having a memory take me by surprise.

So the next time I get the urge to clean out a handbag, I'm going to stop myself.

Because what seems meaningless today could one day be a ticket to a time machine.

Yoga Yokel

LISA

I have no problem admitting when I'm wrong.

And I confess I don't understand people who do.

We're human beings.

We get a free pass on making mistakes.

I make big ones and little ones, and I don't mind admitting it.

For example, I'm divorced twice, from Thing One and Thing Two.

Big mistakes.

When I make a mistake, I'm sorry.

It doesn't kill me to say I'm sorry.

I'm sorry I married Thing One and Thing Two.

The only thing that Thing One ever gave me was Francesca, which makes him my favorite ex-husband.

But believe me, that bar ain't high.

Sorry.

I shouldn't have said that.

See, there you go.

Me making a mistake and then saying I'm sorry, on the very same page!

I'm a professional, folks.

Anyway, one of the other things I like least about myself is that I tend to form an opinion based on almost no facts.

In other words, the fact that I don't know what I'm talking about doesn't stop me from talking.

I call it a gut instinct, or a hunch, but the bottom line is that it's an opinion based on zero.

So let's talk about yoga.

I had views about yoga that made absolutely no sense whatsoever, but I believed them with all my heart.

I confess to you that I would roll my eyes at people who did yoga.

Inwardly.

I would see them in the food store, wearing yoga pants and cute little stretchy tops.

I admit, I was jealous.

And I became a hater.

Of yoga people.

I think I'm not alone in this, and not only about yoga. People decide that an opinion is about their identity, as in, I'm a dog person, not a cat person.

Or I'm a cat person, not a dog person.

It's confusing, because in my case, I'm a cat person and a dog person.

Basically I'm an animal person, which is paradoxical.

Because people also describe me as a people person.

So you get the idea.

That way of thinking doesn't make any sense.

But that's the way I used to think.

I never thought I would do yoga.

I never thought I could do it.

And I never thought I could fit into that much Lycra.

Well.

I'm sorry. I was wrong.

Not about the Lycra.

I'm doing it in sweatpants, but I am actually doing yoga.

Me.

It turns out that there's no such thing as a yoga person.

There was no reason to snark, sniff, or roll my eyes.

What happened was that my good friend Nan started doing it, and she loved it, and so I thought I might love it too.

I decided, I'm going to try yoga.

And I'm here to tell you that I've been doing it for about seven months, twice a week, and I love it.

Okay, before we get carried away, I can't say I love *doing* it.

I'm taking a beginner-level class and it's still really hard.

For those of you who don't know exactly what yoga is, let me break it down for you:

It's a lot of stretching exercises that someone makes you do for reasons you don't quite understand.

And it hurts while you're doing it, but if it hurts too much, you can slack.

You have my permission.

I slack almost the entire class.

For God's sake, I'm doing the class *in* slacks.

But there is no dress code.

And nobody yelled at me.

Because it doesn't matter.

They call slacking "modifications," so let's call it that herein.

As in, I don't slack, I modify.

Take it as a good sign that there's even a word for slacking, which shows you that yoga people aren't the jerks that you thought.

Rather, that I thought.

They're actually really nice.

They're supernice.

That would be the Zen part that will occasionally make you inwardly roll your eyes, until you're the one trying to twist your legs into a pretzel and not fart in someone's face.

Or your own.

Or your ohm.

Namaste.

And I'm here to tell you that I used to have lower back pain, from sitting on my butt all day while I write, and it has completely vanished.

Do you hear me?

Completely *gone.*

And not only that, but you may have read earlier in this book that I tore a hip ligament called the labrum, and it used to hurt every time I raised my leg.

But no longer.

Yoga *cured* me.

Do you believe that?

It's true.

When I went to the orthopedist for a follow-up, I told him I was doing yoga and he said that yoga is the same as physical therapy.

But in my opinion, the music's better.

My orthopedist also told me that he recommends that people do basic yoga to stay fit and flexible.

Who knew?

I didn't.

Don't think that I'm fit and flexible.

But I'm working on it.

And I am pain-free.

And I find myself not wanting to miss the class, which is not like slacker me, who is usually content to skip classes or quit altogether.

Impressed yet?

But not yoga.

It feels like a wonderful stretch all over your body, using muscles you didn't even know you had, but in a calm and slow way. You have time to think about what you're doing, and you learn to pay attention to the way your body feels when you're doing it. And at the end of every class, the last pose you do is resting on the yoga mat with your eyes closed, in an incredibly relaxed state.

That's called Shavasana.

But I call it naptime.

I have fallen asleep twice in class, during Shavasana.

But again, nobody laughs at me.

They just wake me up.

And if I farted while I was asleep, nobody says anything.

Nobody judges.

Everybody is Zen.

My kind of people, after all.

In other words, human beings.

REST IN PEACE, RUBY

LISA

I have very sad news to report, in that our beloved little corgi Ruby has passed away.

She had DM, degenerative myelopathy, which was an increasing paralysis of her little body starting from the back, getting worse over a period of years. She felt no pain because of the illness, but it was finally affecting her ability to breathe. Francesca came home to be with her at the end, and Ruby was put down, peacefully, in our arms.

That is, Ruby was peaceful.

We were hysterical.

Corgis are born to herd, but the fact that there weren't any barnyard animals in the house never stopped Ruby. She herded me, Francesca, the other dogs, and occasionally, even the cat.

Yes, you can herd cats.

If you're a corgi.

She was a small dog with short little legs, which supported a body shaped like a cocktail sausage, but she protected all of us. She saved us by barking at UPS delivery-men, squirrels, and even passing airplanes.

Well, none crashed on me, did they?

I've never had a dog who was so thor-oughly in charge of my house.

For the past fourteen years, she ran the place.

She was small, but so mighty that losing her is a reminder that size really doesn't matter. Nor did her disability or even ill-ness. She had no idea that she was com-pletely incapable of protecting us from anything, yet all of the other dogs obeyed her. Strangers kept their distance.

Occasionally, so did friends.

After her disease paralyzed her back legs, we got her a cart and she raced around the house like a kid on big wheels. She was a terrible driver and ran over everything in her path, including my feet.

I didn't mind.

In time, the disease paralyzed her two front legs, so she couldn't use the cart anymore, but she was happy to lie down on a cushioned pad that we moved wherever we were in the house, sliding her around on it like a magic carpet.

Even then, she would be snapping and nipping at the other dogs, keeping them behind her, so that she could be at the head of the pack.

And they obeyed what was essentially a barking bath mat.

Ruby loved Francesca and me with a ferocity I haven't felt since Mother Mary, and when my mother was alive, she adored Ruby, seeing a kindred spirit in the tiny little dog that ruled the world.

And I will tell you a strange story, because Ruby passed on my mother's birthday, and at the very moment Ruby passed, it began to rain.

On a perfectly sunny day, that wasn't even cloudy.

And after she passed, the rain stopped.

For real.

A five-minute shower on a sunny day.

Every family has its wacky lore, but you may remember that we associate Mother Mary with rain. She always used to joke that she "brings the rain," and also, it poured the day of her funeral, flooding my entrance hall completely.

That hadn't happened before, or since.

So what if it's not completely scientific?

We believe that Mother Mary got Ruby for her birthday.

Because even heaven needs a dog.

We all know by now that you can learn

Ruby and her BFF, Peach

lessons from animals, so many of them that I can't begin to count. But I have never been so inspired by a dog of mine as I was by Ruby.

She lived every day without limits, except those she set for herself.

She was powerful because she believed she was powerful.

She got respect because she settled for nothing less.

And she loved with everything in her little body.

She never left my side or Francesca's, needing neither a leash nor a fence because there was simply nowhere else she wanted to be.

And with her passing, so we have a corgi-shaped hole in our hearts.

We will never forget her.

Or the lessons she taught us.

Or the loyalty she gave us.

Thank you, Ruby.

Now we know something we didn't before.

The smallest of creatures can cast the biggest of shadows.

Depending on the light.

And the love.

In Vino Veritas

LISA

This is where I tell you that I love wine.

As in, love it.

Not that I have a drinking problem.

I have no problem drinking.

It's like eating.

It comes naturally to me.

Also I get a lot of practice.

Before I begin, let me say up front that I'm not joking about a serious drinking problem. I know that alcoholism exists, and I have known people who have struggled with addiction to alcohol. But I'm talking about an occasional wine with dinner, and I trust you, my brilliant readers, to know the difference.

You came here for the laughs.

I aim to deliver.

In fact, I hope you're drinking right now.

The more you drink, the funnier I get.

I always think this when I do speaking engagements, which are held after a nice dinner has been served.

I take the lectern, giving people ample time to order a second bottle of wine "for the table."

That's one of my favorite phrases, by the way.

The Flying Scottolines always ordered wine for the table, along with an extra appetizer, entrée, and dessert, also for the table.

Evidently, the table eats a lot.

And the table loved wine.

I often wondered if the table could drink itself under the table.

Because it definitely had a wooden leg.

Anyway, back to my speaking engagement, where I take the lectern, tell my stories, and they all drink and drink and laugh and laugh.

Afterwards they tell me what a great speaker I am.

I always say, Hurray for Chardonnay!

Anyway, as you may know, my family is Italian-American, so we're no stranger to wine. Growing up, we drank wine with dinner occasionally and we always had wine at a holiday meal, even when we were young.

It wasn't a big deal, so it never got in the forbidden-fruit category.

But don't get the opposite impression,

that it was fancy.

We never drank anything but red wine.

And it was always served in a water glass.

I distinctly remember having Flintstones jelly glasses when I was little, and I would have my wine in a Flintstones glass.

Nowadays, they would call child services.

But it was just Christmas at the Scottolines'.

In fact, my grandmother on my father's side made her own wine in the basement of her rowhome in West Philadelphia. She had a wooden winepress that I have to this very day, in my backyard, to remember her by.

That would be the sum total of my inheritance.

And the wine she made was terrific, but not in the sense of a wine snob. It was probably Chianti, or at least a red wine that wanted to be Chianti. It was heavy enough to float a tanker and thick enough to dye your teeth red. In every holiday picture, the Scottolines look like vampires.

A few years ago, I decided I was going to try winemaking myself, so I bought the grapes at a place in New Jersey, mashed them, and tried to distill my own wine in a massive jar in the basement, which had a thin glass pipe coming out of the top like a curlicue Krazy Straw.

The bottom line was I'm no bootlegger.

And my entire house smelled like a salad.

As I grew up, I became vaguely intimidated by wines, since the world has become replete with wine snobs.

But I've learned to ignore them.

And I've settled on my one variety of wine that I absolutely adore.

It's the least fancy and most downmarket of all.

Lambrusco.

It's served cold, and it's bubbly and sweet, which is the most refreshing drink for a summer evening.

If you like Welch's grape juice, you'll love Lambrusco.

Lambrusco is fun in a bottle, and one glass improves everything about the world.

I don't know what happens after one glass because if I have more than one, I fall asleep.

So I'm a happy, if sleepy, drunk.

And the other great thing about Lambrusco is that it's among the cheapest wines. Even the best bottle costs twelve bucks.

So you can save money.

I'm literally my own cheap drunk.

I'll drink to that!

■ ■ ■ ■

A Decade of Chick Wit: Special Bonus Section

■ ■ ■ ■

All God's creatures have an origin story, and so does this series of books. Below is the explanation for how these books came to be, but I can give you the executive summary, from the horse's mouth. If you're reading these in book form, you are reading something that started life as a newspaper column for *The Philadelphia Inquirer,* over a decade ago. Francesca and I write a Sunday column which is entitled "Chick Wit," and it has evolved over the years, but we've always kept it funny, bright, and a true story of mothers and daughters, or of women living their lives and getting into normal female trouble, as opposed to felonious. But these books are the highest and best form of our true-life stories, because they contain many stories that haven't been printed before, whether because we can't, or we won't, or we just want to write something very special for all of you. So below is a sampling of our greatest hits that you may not have read before, which we include as a special thank-you to our most loyal readers. Enjoy, and read on!

A Decade of Chick Wit

LISA

It's amazing to think that "Chick Wit" has run for ten whole years.

Especially since I haven't aged a day.

I was barely a chick when it started.

So maybe it's time to explain how it hatched.

Enough with the metaphor.

Metaphors are never funny.

You know what's funny?

Spanx.

Anyway, the column started when one day, I was sitting at my kitchen table reading the *Inquirer,* and all the news was bad.

There was nothing funny.

And I started to remember the funny columnists I grew up reading, who wrote about their real lives, like Erma Bombeck.

I thought, maybe I can bring the funny.

Long story short, I begged the *Inky* to let me do a column, and they agreed, thanks to former owner Brian Tierney.

I started writing about my life and my daughter Francesca, so in time she joined the column to write about life from her perspective.

And to write about me.

Yikes.

That would strike fear into any mother's heart, but as Francesca and I always say to each other, "If it doesn't make us cringe, it won't make them laugh."

So for ten years, we've covered major life events in our family, like Francesca's college graduation, where I cried so hard someone thought I was drunk. And the passing of our beloved Mother Mary. I would say, may she rest in peace, but that wasn't her style.

She's raising hell. In heaven.

We wrote about our neighbor Harry, who used to join us for Thanksgiving dinner. And how after his death, we took in his cat Spunky, who was reportedly on his last four legs.

And who proceeded to live for six very expensive years.

Francesca wrote about making eggplant with Mother Mary and losing me in NYC. I wrote about going braless to the emergency room and my crush on Brad Pitt, before I moved on to George Clooney and ultimately to Bradley Cooper.

And now he's having my baby.

Oh, wait.

So you would think "Chick Wit" is a column about us, but it isn't.

It's about you.

Though we write about ourselves, Mother Mary, and our dogs, we've always been writing in our representative capacity as people with ovaries.

Women.

"Chick Wit" is not for women, but it is about them.

That's why the column connects with people, if I may say so.

People relate to it because it's like their own lives. We get email every day from readers who say, "I have a Mother Mary too," or "I crave carbs too," or "I love fleece too, especially if it has an elastic waistband."

Okay, I made up that last one.

But you get the point.

If you ask me what I'm proudest of, it's that for the past decade, we have gotten to write a column about you. Because you, too, have lived through graduations, losses, and the ups and downs of everyday living in family, of whatever size and shape.

Now you can open a newspaper and laugh.

At us!

And at the same time, you can see yourselves, your daughters, your dogs, and your cats represented in *The Philadelphia Inquirer*.

You all deserve to be the headlines, as far as we're concerned.

"Chick Wit" matters because families matter, and sometimes we need a reminder of the smaller things in life, because what happens around the breakfast table is just as important as what happens in Washington, D.C.

If not more so.

And to my mind, we need not only to laugh, but to remember our commonalities. We're more divided than ever, with Republicans and Democrats splintering along different ideological lines. Constructive dialogue has dipped to an all-time low. Everywhere you turn, there's something to remind you of how different you are from someone else.

But this, too, shall pass.

You know what abides?

Love.

Family.

Laughter.

It's good to remember that we are, in fact, the same under the skin.

And if we're lucky, we all have a crazy family that we like to make fun of.

And hug.

And fight with.

Thank you, readers, for sharing a decade of laughs!

And make up with.

And live and die with.

So here's to the next decade of this wonderful life, together.

Thanks so much to the *Inquirer* for its support of "Chick Wit."

But more importantly, thanks so much to all of you.

We are forever grateful.

LISA'S FAVORITE COLUMN
OF FRANCESCA'S

My favorite column of Francesca's is "Love Without Rough Edges." She chose to write about one of the most difficult and painful subjects, the loss of her beloved grandmother, Mother Mary, and she did so in a way that was original and poignant. Francesca took wonderful care of Mother Mary in hospice, and you can tell that they had a special relationship in every line of this column. Generally we hear a lot about how important grandchildren are from a grandparent's point of view, but it's equally wonderful to hear how important grandparents are to their grandchildren, to the very end.

LOVE WITHOUT ROUGH EDGES
FRANCESCA

Last week, we lost our beloved Mother Mary. She passed peacefully at home, without pain, surrounded by all of us. It still hardly feels real to me, so it isn't easy to write about. My head, and my heart, aren't ready to put her in the past tense.

I feel lucky I was able to be with her for the last weeks she was home with us. I tried to help however I could and keep her company the rest of the time. But hospice is a game you play to lose, and it was difficult to adjust.

Often, I felt helpless.

So when my uncle said that my grandmother had specifically asked for me to do her nails, I was elated — unlike the daunting medical side of hospice, this was something I knew I could handle.

My grandmother took meticulous care of her fingernails. She always carried an emery board in her handbag, and even when her knuckles knotted with arthritis, she kept each filed to a perfect almond shape.

Even now, she could feel her nails were long, but she couldn't feel the advanced cancer in her chest.

One of many blessings.

So I was happy to help. I envisioned giving her a salon experience, complete with soaking bowls of warm, sudsy water and a hand massage with scented lotion. I wanted so badly to do something nice for her, something special.

When you know that anything could be the last something, you want everything to be perfect.

But the next morning, I could see she was exhausted, more so than the day before.

It takes a lot for a body to launch a spirit.

Especially one like hers.

I put my hand on her shoulder as she napped on the couch. "Is it all right if I do your nails while you rest?"

She opened her eyes for a moment and gave a nod.

I took her hands one by one, my fingers threaded through hers. I filed each nail gently, so as not to disturb her, rounding the tips into half-moons. I ran my fingers over them to make sure they were perfectly clean and smooth, no rough edges.

I thought of all these hands had done in ninety years. Before my time, she was a songwriter, her hands played many melodies on piano. I imagined her penciling in the margins of a new song, adding dynamic changes, a *ritardando* at the end.

If only there was a *ritardando* in real life. But you can't hold on to one minute longer than any other. And the more you try, the faster they seem to go.

I thought of all these hands had done for me. How many meals had they prepared? How many other babysitters served home-made ravioli as an after-school snack? How many times had they stroked my hair? Touched my cheek? How many gestures of love can a lifetime hold?

In my grandmother's case, countless.

So I held on to her hands while she slept. And I whispered to her, told her things, some important and mundane, some I'd said a thousand times before, some I'd never said 'til then.

I hoped she could feel in my hands the love returned to her, the lessons learned, the strength she'd instilled in me now trying to be strong for her.

I always admired my grandmother's combination of grit and warmth, she could be tough and tender, hard and soft.

Although she was all soft with me.

She loved without rough edges.

After some time she woke up, or maybe she hadn't been asleep at all, and she ran her thumb over her fingertips. She smiled. "Good," she told me, and she blew me a kiss.

I wondered if she had heard me say that I loved her enough to hope she could let go.

Even though I wanted to hold her hands awhile longer.

Column with the Greatest Readers' Reaction

"Everything Old Is Nude Again" is the column that people stop me on the street and say they remember. That makes me so happy because I think this column exemplifies the true spirit of "Chick Wit." We like to write funny stories about everyday, relatable problems like trying to fit into your jeans — or worse, your Spanx. These stories may not be the stuff of headlines, but they are the stuff of life.

Everything Old
Is Nude Again

LISA

Something dangerous is going on in the world of women's underwear, and I want to nip it in the butt.

Sorry.

I am referring, of course, to Spanx.

If you don't know what Spanx are, I have one word for you:

Girdles.

I got introduced to Spanx by accident, when I bought a black-patterned pair, thinking they were tights. I got my size, which is B.

For Beautiful.

I took them home and put them on, which was like slipping into a tourniquet. Then I realized they weren't tights, they were just Tight, and I checked the box, which read Tight-End Tights.

Huh?

I actually managed to squeeze myself into them, then I put on a knit dress, examined myself in the mirror, and hated what I saw. From the front, I looked like a Tootsie Roll with legs. From the back, instead of having buttocks, I had buttock.

In other words, my lower body had been transformed into a cylinder. I no longer had hips where hips are supposed to be, or saddlebags where God intended. I was the cardboard in the roll of toilet paper.

And another detail — I couldn't breathe.

Also the elastic waistband was giving me a do-it-yourself hysterectomy.

I didn't understand the product, so I went instantly to the website, which explained that these were no ordinary tights but were "slimming apparel." This, under the bright pink banner that read, "It's what's on the inside that counts!"

Really?

The website claimed that "these innovative undergarments eliminate VBL (visible bra lines) and VPL (visible panty lines)."

Well.

Would this be a good time to say that I'm in favor of VBL and VPL? Especially VPL. In fact, I want my P as V as possible.

You know why?

Because I wear P.

I don't know what kind of signal we're sending if we want our butts to suggest otherwise. Bottom line, I'm not the kind of girl who goes without P. In other words, I'm a Good Girl (GG). And GGs wear P.

Same goes for B.

I admit, I get a little lazy, especially at home or in the emergency room. I don't always bother with B all the time. But if I'm in public and not wearing a down coat, I wear B. And I also want my B to be V.

You know why?

I want extra credit.

If I went to the trouble to put on a B, I want to be recognized for it. Here's an analogy; I'm not the kind of person who makes charitable donations anonymously. If I give away money, I want a plaque or maybe a stadium named after me, so everybody knows that I'm nice, in addition to being good. (N and G). In fact, that makes me a N and GG.

But back to P and B.

I went back to the mirror and noticed

something else — that the fat that properly belonged on my hips, having taken up residence there at age 40, was now home-less and being relocated upward by my tights, leaving a roll at my waist which could pass for a flotation device.

But have no fear. I checked the website, and Spanx has the solution: "slimming camis." That is, camisoles that look like Ace bandages, which presumably pick up the fat roll at the waist and squeeze it upward, so that, having nowhere else to go, it pops out on top, as breasts.

Ta-da!

Or rather, ta-tas!

This is interesting, for physics. Natural law says that matter cannot be created or destroyed, but that was pre-Spanx. With these babies, you could destroy the matter at your waistline and increase it at your bustline, merely by turning your body into a half-squeezed tube of toothpaste.

And of course, you'll need a new bra to catch all your homeless fat, so the website sells "the Bra-llelujah!" It even states, "So, say goodbye to BBS (Bad Bra Syndrome)!"

Thank God. I hate it when my B is B.

I looked at the other articles of slimming apparel, and there were even tights for pregnant women, which was great. I wouldn't want my baby to be born with VIL (Visible Infant Lines).

And there were Power Panties, which made me smile.

If women had power, they wouldn't need Spanx.

BEST MOTHER-DAUGHTER COLUMN

There are some issues unique to the mother-daughter relationship, okay, a lot of issues. Years later, readers still mention this column and tell me, "OMG, you're *me,*" and "That's *my* mom." It feels good to know we're all in this together! And while I'd like to say I've gotten better at talking to my mom, you know what they say, the more things change . . . the more moms worry.

HOW TO TALK TO MOMS

FRANCESCA

Did you hear about the ten-year-old who writes self-help books? His name is Alec Greven, and he penned, or crayoned, *How to Talk to Moms.* Presumably, the intended audience is other ten-year-olds, but I think this book could have broader appeal.

Namely, me.

I wasn't attracted to it in some condescending, look-how-cute way either. I need this book. I need help figuring out How to Talk to Mom.

But here's the problem. I need the twenty-four-year-old-just-moved-out version.

As you know, my mom and I are very close. When it comes to the big issues, feelings, emotions, etc., I can always speak frankly with Mom. It's the small stuff I'm sweating.

For instance, last night, I went to see my cousin in Long Island City. No big deal. So I mentioned this mundane outing matter-of-factly to my mother over the phone. But as a matter of fact, she didn't find it so mundane.

"How are you getting there? The subway? At night? ALONE?"

I thought I said, "I am going to see Paul's new apartment," but in mom-speak that translates to: "I am going to meet certain death in the New York City subway tunnels that are soon to be my tomb."

Talk about lost in translation.

So how should I have said this to avoid throwing Mom into an unrecoverable tailspin of fear and worry?

Recently, I met a nice guy while out at a bar with friends. He's a young lawyer and it turns out he grew up near me and we have a lot in common. I gave him my number and lo and behold, he actually called me to go out. I share this good news with Mom, but again, in plain English. Her response?

"Dinner with a stranger? Did you verify what he told you? He could be anyone, you have no way of knowing."

See, my story in Mom-ese translated to "I

met a guy named Ted Bundy, and I think he really likes me!"

To appease her, I had to Google the guy, find his last five addresses, proof of his alleged alma mater, and one official Notice of Appearance in court to prove he was a practicing (she immediately assumed he was laid-off) lawyer. And she still wanted me to spring for the $19.95 criminal background check.

I didn't.

God help me the night I actually went on the date.

I understand playing it safe, so my mother and I discussed some strategies on how to protect myself *just in case.* Meet him at the restaurant instead of my apartment, make sure I get in the cab to go home alone, tell my roommate where I'm going and plan when she should call me and expect me back, etc. I thought I had said all the right things in my pre-date Talk With Mom. But I made one critical error, this time, not with what I said, but what I did NOT say.

I did not say, "I'll call you when I'm home."

Big mistake.

Like, huge.

You see, New York dinners start kind of late, so I was still out at 11:00 P.M. when she texted the first time. And the bar we went to afterwards was loud, so I didn't hear my phone ring at 11:37 P.M. or again around midnight. And we happened to have a conversation about how people who constantly check their Blackberries are so annoying, so I kept it in my purse while the four other text messages chimed in. And at the very end of the date, the guy actually seemed to want to kiss me, so when I finally did hear my ringer go off, I quickly silenced it and leaned in.

Kiss of death.

In the cab I saw I had five new text messages, three missed calls, and two new voice mails. I winced when I listened to the first voice mail and heard my mom's barely controlled voice saying, "Hi, honey. Just making sure you're okay. Please call me when you get home."

But this time, I could translate.

"CALL ME NOW I AM FREAKING OUT!"

I felt terrible. Sure, my mom was over-reacting a little (I found out when I did call her that she had even emailed my roommate). But the fact remained that for a couple hours there, she was really scared for me, and all because of a simple break-down of communication.

So how does the newly-moved-out twenty-something talk to Mom?
Alec Greven can't grow up fast enough.

Never underestimate a mother — and if she's a grandmother, take cover! It was hard to choose, but I think this is my favorite of all my mom's columns. I love it because she captured the powerful force that was Mother Mary, with all her spunk, determination, and a dose of magic. And I love it because, perhaps without realizing it, my mom captured the greatest lesson both of these powerful women passed down to me: never underestimate yourself.

Earthquake Mary

LISA

I am a mother, I have a mother, and I love mothers. I think mothers are a natural force, and maybe an alternative source of fuel.

Observe.

My mother, Mother Mary, lives with Brother Frank in South Beach. She awoke one morning with a start, convinced that her bed had moved during sleep, as if there had been an earthquake. But nothing was out of place in her bedroom, and it was a cloudless Sunday, still as a postcard. Nevertheless, she was sure there had been an earthquake. She went and woke up my brother, who told her to go back to sleep.

She didn't. She scurried across the street like an octogenarian Chicken Little, to warn their neighbor. He told her to go back to sleep, too.

Instead she went home and called the *Miami Herald.*

She told the reporter about the earthquake, and he told her that the sky wasn't falling and suggested she go back to sleep. He also took her name and telephone number, which turned out to be a good thing, because he had to call her back, later that day.

She had been absolutely right. There had been an earthquake, at the exact time she had felt it.

The clincher? The earthquake occurred 397 miles from Miami, in Tampa. And the only person who felt it in Miami was my mother, Mary Scottoline.

I'm not kidding.

Soon, TV newsvans began arriving at my mother's house. My brother, who you may remember is gay, told me he put on his "best tank top."

The Scottolines have style.

The reporters interviewed my mother, and under her picture on the TV screen, the banner read EARTHQUAKE MARY. They asked her how she felt an earthquake that took place so far away. She answered that she "knows about these things."

The *Miami Herald* published the story, as reported by Martin Merzer and Aldo Nahed. My favorite part reads, "It was a pretty nice weekend in Florida. Except, you know, for the 6.0 magnitude earthquake . . . In South Florida, the event passed virtually unnoticed, though Mary Scottoline, 82 . . ."

If you don't believe me, go and find the story online. Google "Mary Scottoline." Or "I-Told-You-I'm-Not-Crazy Scottoline," "Nobody-Ever-Listens-To-Me Scottoline," or "You-And-Your-Brother-Think-You-Know-Everything-with-that-Cockamamie-Computer Scottoline."

It wasn't the first time that Mother Mary had something in common with a natural disaster. Once I made her fly north to me to avoid a hurricane, and she wasn't happy about it. When she got off the plane, a TV reporter stuck a microphone in her face and asked if she was afraid of the hurricane. She answered:

"I'm not afraid of a hurricane. I *am* a hurricane."

So you see what we're dealing with. A force of nature. A four-foot-eleven bundle of heart, bile, and moxie.

And superpowers.

I've known for a long time that Mother Mary has superpowers. She used to cast off the evil eye when somebody gave me a "whammy," by chanting a secret spell over a bowl of water and olive oil. She dipped her fingers in the water, made the sign of the cross on my forehead, and whispered mysterious words that sounded like *osso bucco.* This spell was handed down to her by another Italian Mother/Witch on Christmas Eve, which is the only time it can be told. She won't tell me the spell because I'm a lawyer.

But I digress.

Your mother may not smear olive oil on your face, but she has superpowers, too. Spider-Man has nothing on mothers.

We don't think of mothers as having superpowers, but they do. Mothers can tell what we're doing when their backs are turned to us. They know we have a fever without a thermometer. They can be at three places at once, a soccer game, a violin lesson, and the high school play, even if it's *Annie.* They can tell we're sad by the way we say, "I'm fine."

And, magically, they can change us into them, without us even knowing how or when. Mother Mary used to make me call her when I got home and let the phone ring three times, as a signal. (This, in a time when long-distance calls cost money.) I thought it was silly, but she said, "When you're a mother, you'll understand."

And finally, I do.

ACKNOWLEDGMENTS

LISA AND FRANCESCA

Time for thank-yous! We love and thank St. Martin's Press for supporting this entire series from day one to bestsellerdom. The biggest thanks go to Coach Jen Enderlin, our terrific editor, and major thanks to the brilliant John Sargent, Don Weisberg, Sally Richardson, Jeff Dodes, Jeff Capshew, Lisa Senz, Brant Janeway, Erica Martirano, Tom Thompson, Jordan Hanley, John Karle, George Witte, John Edwards, Jeanette Zwart, Dori Weintraub, Tracey Guest, Stephanie Davis, Brian Heller, Brad Wood, Michael Storrings, Anne-Marie Tallberg, Kerry Nordling, Elizabeth Wildman, Talia Sherer, Kim Ludlum, Rachel Diebel, and all the wonderful sales reps. We appreciate you all!

We'd also like to thank St. Martin's audiobook division for letting us record our own audiobook of this volume, which we love doing. Thanks to the terrific Mary Beth

Roche, our director Laura Wilson, and Samantha Edelson. We love audiobooks!

Huge thanks and love to Lisa's amazing agent, Robert Gottlieb of the Trident Media Group, and his awesome digital team, Nicole Robson, Caitlin O'Beirne, Diana Rodon, and Alicia Granstein. Equally huge thanks and love to Francesca's terrific agents, Andrea Cirillo, Amy Tannenbaum, and Rebecca Scherer of the Jane Rotrosen Agency — you are guiding lights. Thanks to *The Philadelphia Inquirer,* which carries our "Chick Wit" column, and to our editors, Reid Tuvim and Alison Smith.

One of the best people in the whole entire world is our bestie/honorary aunt/resident therapist/genius assistant Laura Leonard. Laura, thank you so much for all of your great comments and suggestions to these stories. We owe you and love you, forever.

Love to our girlfriends! Lisa would like to thank Nan Daley, Paula Menghetti, Sandy Steingard, and Franca Palumbo. Francesca would like to thank Rebecca Harrington, Katy Andersen, Courtney Yip, Lauren Donahoe, Janie Stolar, and right-hand man, Ryder Kessler. We're blessed in all of you.

Family is the heart of this book, because family is the heart of everything. Special thanks and love to Brother Frank. We still miss Mother Mary and Father Frank Scottoline, though they are with us always.

Finally, a massive thank-you to our readers. You have taken this series to your heart, and so touched ours. Nothing makes us happier.

We are truly honored.

ABOUT THE AUTHORS

Lisa Scottoline is a *New York Times* best-selling and Edgar Award–winning novelist and coauthor of this series of humorous memoirs. There are 30 million copies of her novels in print, and she has been published in thirty countries. She and Francesca also write a Sunday column entitled "Chick Wit" for *The Philadelphia Inquirer*. She lives in the Philadelphia suburbs with an array of disobedient pets. You can visit Lisa at scotto line.com.

Francesca Serritella is a *New York Times* bestselling author and a columnist for *The Philadelphia Inquirer*. She graduated cum laude from Harvard University, where she won the Thomas Temple Hoopes Prize for her novella. She lives in New York City with one dog and one cat, so far, and she is working on a novel. You can visit Francesca at francescaserritella.com.